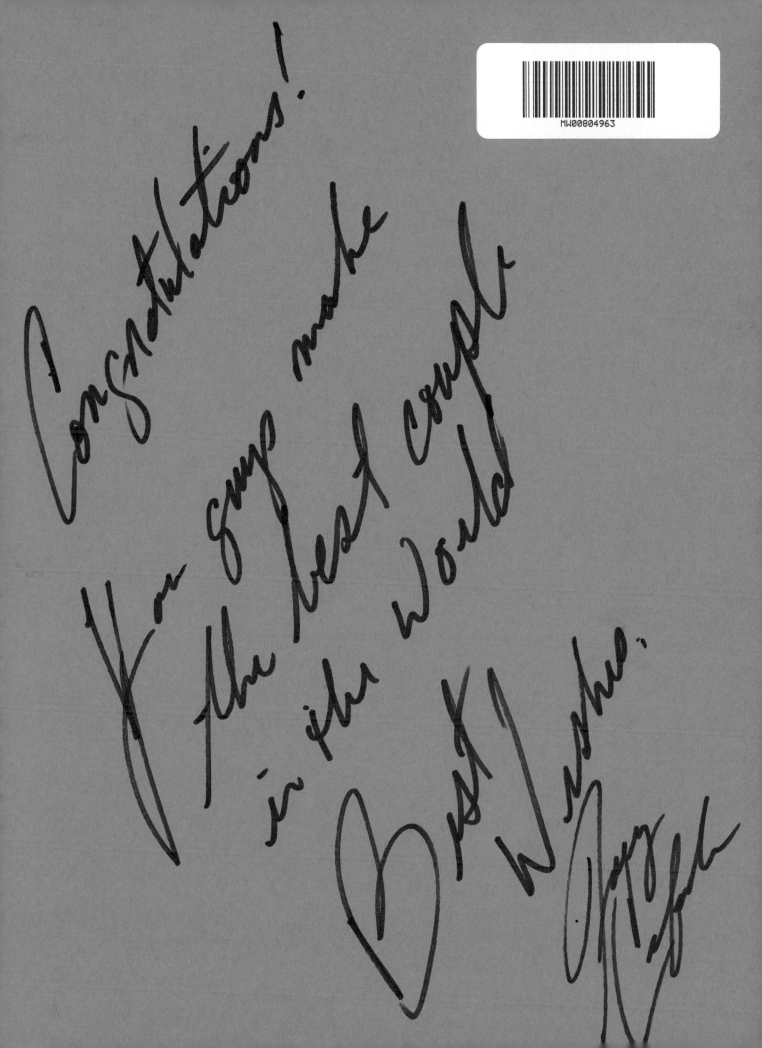

Congratulations!

For guys made the best couple in the world

Best Wishes.

# III FORKS

The III Forks dining experience is like no other. The excitement begins with the first glimpse of this magnificent structure, like something straight from *Arabian Nights…*

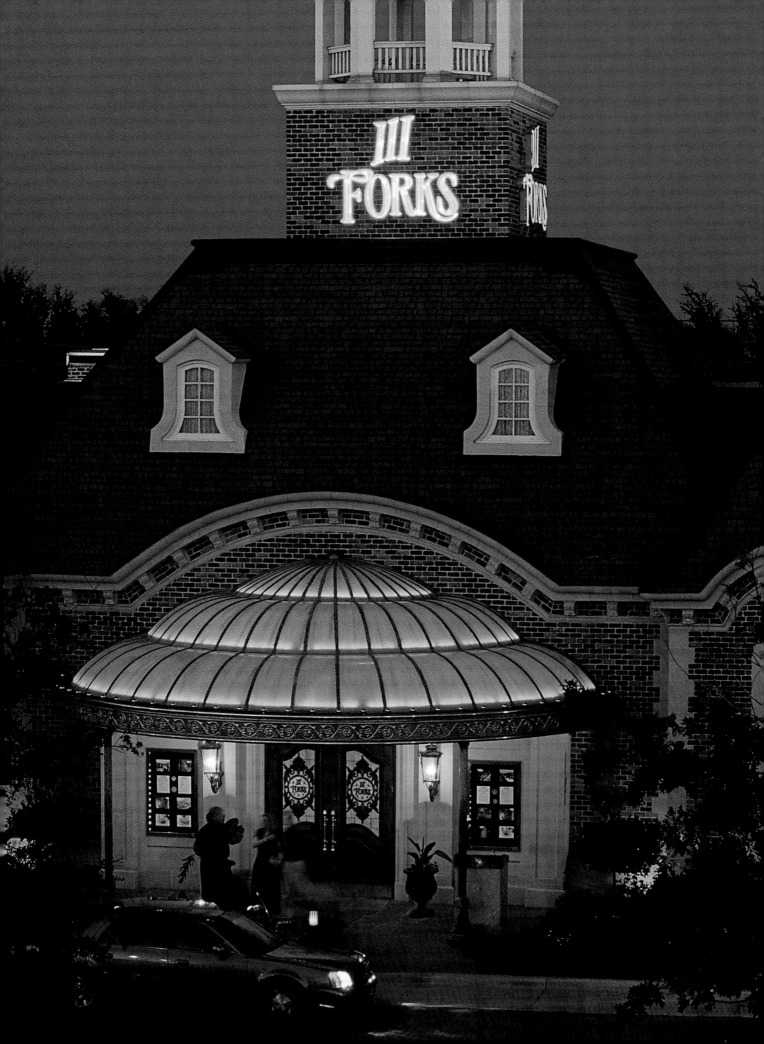

# III FORKS

## An Insider's Look at the Famed Restaurant and Its Cuisine

### Whit Smyth

Photographs by Jay Brousseau

LEBHAR-FRIEDMAN BOOKS

NEW YORK • CHICAGO • LOS ANGELES • LONDON • PARIS • TOKYO

*THIS BOOK IS DEDICATED TO THE MEMORY OF OUR FRIEND,*

*WARREN F. LERUTH, MAY 11, 1929 — NOVEMBER 7, 2001*

LEBHAR-FRIEDMAN BOOKS
A company of Lebhar-Friedman, Inc.
425 Park Avenue
New York, New York 10022

Great Restaurants of the World® is a trademark of Lebhar-Friedman Books

LIBRARY OF CONGRESS CATALOGING-IN-PUBLICATION DATA
Cataloging-in-publication data for this title is on file with the Library of Congress.
ISBN 0-86730-915-6

*Designed and composed by Kevin Hanek,*
*based on an original series design by Nancy Koch, NK Design*

Manufactured in the United States of America on acid-free paper.
*Visit our Web site at lfbooks.com*

WHIT SMYTH is the senior copywriter for Madigan & McManus, Inc., a Stamford, Connecticut marketing agency that specializes in the publishing industry. Clients include *Nation's Restaurant News,* a publication of Lebhar-Friedman, Inc.  A former reporter with the *Baltimore Sun,* Smyth is also a freelance writer. His book, *Great Taste Endures: The Story of Arby's Restaurants,* was published by Lebhar-Friedman Books in 1999. Smyth lives in Kingston Springs, Tennessee, with his wife, Shari, a contributing editor for *Guideposts* magazine. They have four grown children.

JAY BROUSSEAU brings concepts and messages to life through his photography. A native Texan, Brousseau has operated a commercial studio in Dallas for more than 20 years, capturing award-winning images of everything from leaders of business and industry to aerials and architecture, including, of course, restaurants. His work has been published in more than 30 countries and he recently completed a project for an electronics manufacturer which took him to Korea and China. Jay's clients include Fortune 500 corporations, advertising agencies, book publishers, and numerous magazines.

ALSO IN THE *GREAT RESTAURANTS OF THE WORLD* SERIES

# Contents

# FOREWORD

Few experiences in life enhance the joy of living more than a fine dining experience. The ambience, style, service, food, and presentation of a great restaurant are all elements that add immensely to enjoying a culinary adventure. Many restaurants provide customers with a consistent dining experience, and a number of these are truly outstanding. Only a few, however, exceed the expectations of even their most discerning patrons. They deserve to be called great, and we are proud to recognize them as Great Restaurants of the World. We are pleased to introduce this latest addition to the series, which already includes:

Café des Artistes
Charlie Trotter's
Commander's Palace
The Inn at Little Washington
The Sardine Factory

These beautiful books have been a labor of love and dedication for all the parties involved. We have called upon the editors of *Nation's Restaurant News,* the leading business publication serving the restaurant industry, to assist us in developing the criteria for the Great Restaurants of the World series and in choosing the candidates. We think you will agree that the selection are of great interest and merit.

All of the Great Restaurants of the World represent a unique creative spirit of providing the public with a meaningful dining experience. However, they also share many of the same traits. Most significantly, each was founded by one or more persons with the kind of entrepreneurial energy dedicated to achieving excellence. Without exception, these founders instilled in their organizations a single compelling mission: to provide their guests with the ultimate dining experience. Food and food presentation are always first priority. After that come service, ambience, and value.

All of these restaurants have been successful by paying attention to innumerable small details every day, every week, and every month throughout the year. Each has proved many times over its reputation as a truly great restaurant through the loyalty of it's repeat customers and the steady stream of awards and recognition it has received over the years, both from its guests and from its peers.

This book and the others in the series are your invitation to experience the Great Restaurants of the World, their history and their heritage. Savor every page and enjoy the adventure.

James C. Doherty
Executive Vice-President
Lebhar-Friedman, Inc.

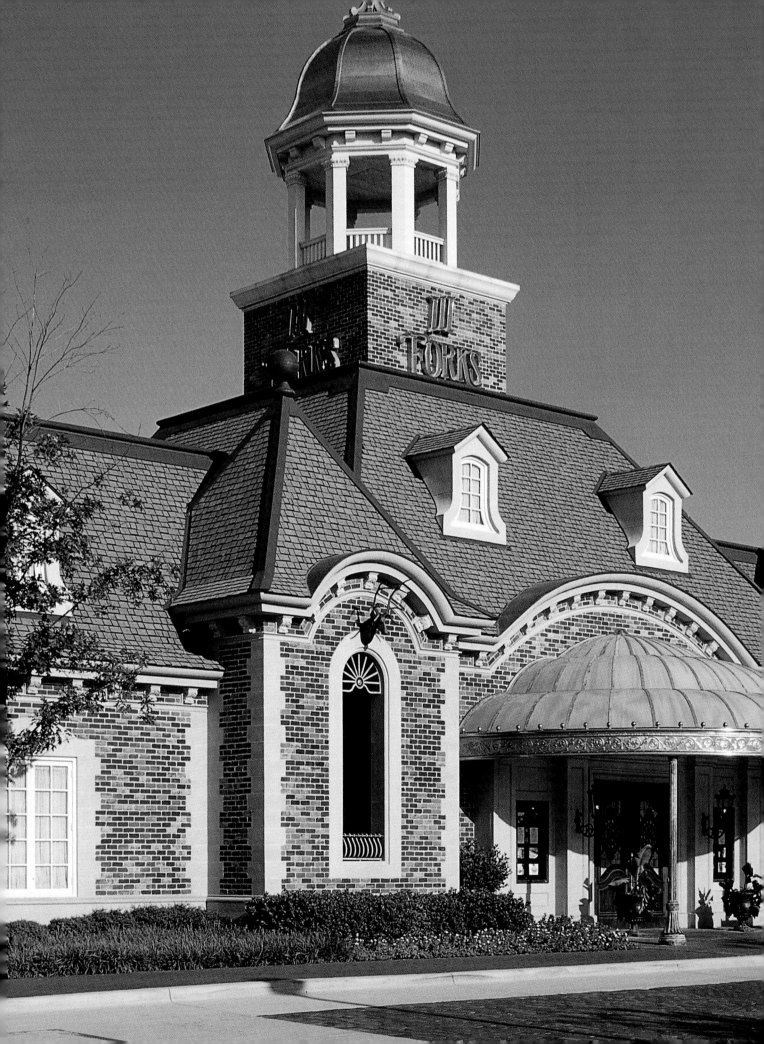

# *III Forks*

CHAPTER ONE

# An Extraordinary Experience

The III Forks restaurant dining experience is like no other. The excitement begins with the first glimpse of this magnificent structure, its white cupola topped by a shimmering 24-karat gold dome. It's like something straight from *Arabian Nights,* hinting at intrigue, adventure, and excitement.

And excitement is what a visitor first feels when entering III Forks. The splendor begins in the lobby. This easily could be mistaken for a fine hotel with its oriental carpets, stained-glass ceilings, elaborate wall lighting, and buzz of activity. A six-foot world globe stands majestically in the center, a subtle reminder that III Forks might, at least for this night, be the center of the diner's universe.

To the right, a curving mahogany bar beckons. To the left lies a hallway leading to an airy courtyard dining room with elegant fountains. Straight ahead is the Lafayette Room, a 90-seat main dining area with a fire that burns constantly in the hearth, and where guests can socialize.

With 12 separate dining rooms on two levels, III Forks is spacious but not overwhelming thanks to subdued lighting that casts a cozy glow.

"Oh, it's big alright, and people often ask, 'Where's my hotel room,'" says Assistant Manager Stacy Hawkins with a chuckle. Every night she greets guests as they enter Dale Wamstad's fabulous steak and seafood restaurant in North Dallas.

"If I had to describe III Forks, I would say it's awe-some and energetic," says Pamela Landgraf, the restaurant's National Director of Sales. "This place hums."

Office Manager Tierney Jory loves the way people react. "When someone who's never been here before walks in, they're just in awe at the size, the grandeur, the stained glass, the huge bar area, and everyone bustling about."

This is the feel that the 60-year-old Wamstad set out to create when he envisioned III Forks in the mid-1990s. "I believe, if you enter a place for the first time, you get an immediate feeling if you're going to like it. So I want to knock your socks off."

III Forks will do that. Yes it's big—25,000 square feet, 12 dining rooms and seating for from 10 to 1,000. But it's also warm. There's an intimacy about the place. Perhaps it's the friendly welcome from front-of-house employees like Hawkins and General Manager Rick Stein, or the smiles and "How are you tonight?" greetings from the waitstaff. Maybe it's the distinctive touches like the world globe just waiting to be examined and twirled, or the clipper ship model in the display cabinet, and the shoeshine stand in the main corridor.

Whatever the reason, III Forks quickly draws you in. Warmth replaces bigness. Delight replaces awe.

"My personal philosophy is the same as Dale's. You talk to every table, you reach every customer," says Stein.

With an average of 800 guests a night, that can be a daunting task, taking up to 45 minutes to circulate through the two-story restaurant. But at III Forks there's no substitute for details, from small amenities like a personal greeting and constantly refilled water glasses, to show stoppers like fresh food served right from the broiler.

"If I didn't say 'hi' when you came in or were seated, I make it my business to come by when your dinner comes out," adds Stein, a former waiter and bartender at fine dining restaurants. One of his stops was Del Frisco's in

# III Forks quickly draws you in. Warmth replaces bigness. Delight replaces awe.

Dallas where he met Wamstad, the creator and driving force behind that successful steak house concept.

When Wamstad started building III Forks in 1996, he studiously avoided copying Del Frisco's. "From the mirrors to the paintings to the food, we did everything differently. For example, we have a full menu here instead of a la carte, unlike other steak houses."

That menu, featuring Texas French cuisine, reflects the difference. All entrees are served with a melt-in-your-mouth potato and perfectly-tex-tured vegetables, fresh ripe tomatoes, and spring onions. The "Beef Market" side of the menu offers tender prime sirloin and filet mignon, bone-in ribeye, porterhouse, succulent III Forks pepper steak, tender-loin tips, baby rack of lamb and veal rib chop. III Forks is one of the few prime steak houses in America that serves exclu-sively prime beef.

Equally impressive is the "Fish Market" side with scrumptious fried shrimp and other tantalizing favorites like trout pecan, Dover sole, salmon, sea bass, scallops, and lobster tails.

Then there's the Crabcake St. Francis. "They have the finest crabcake in the coun-try that I've eaten by far," says Warren Leruth, the noted menu consultant and renown chef from Louisiana who has advised Wamstad on numerous occasions through the years.

Everything at III Forks is made fresh. Nothing is pre-cooked and there are no warmers. No food is prepared until a guest orders it. "There's an honesty, a purity that's at the heart of everything we do," says Wamstad.

"We make everything here but the butter," says award-winning Execu-tive Chef Chris Vogeli. "We bake our own breads. We make our own desserts and homemade ice cream. Our beef is the finest you can buy, and

our seafood is flown in fresh daily. That's no easy task when you're open seven days a week."

In addition to offering the finest in fresh beef and seafood, Wamstad wanted a big restaurant that would serve hundreds of dinner guests each night and also be a magnet for corporate meetings, banquets, birthday parties, and weddings.

"There was a need for this in the Dallas area," he adds. "We want III Forks to be an experience. We want you to feel good here."

Wamstad's wife, Colleen, thinks the entire feel of III Forks is lighter and less masculine than your typical steak house. "It doesn't just appeal to a business clientele, but to everyone, including families."

Opened in August 1998, the restaurant sits on five acres just off the Tollway about 20 minutes from downtown Dallas. Sales reached $11 million in 2000, an 11% increase over 1999.

While III Forks did better from day one than Wamstad had anticipated, the early weeks were no picnic for this perfectionist. In fact, it took six months for the operation to settle down and become what he had in mind. Today, the silver-haired restaurateur loves the feeling he gets every night when he walks through the elaborate stained-glass front doors.

"Normally when a restaurant opens up you have either a strong kitchen and a weak dining room, or vice versa," he explains. "But when they're both strong and mesh together, it's a beautiful thing."

Creating a people-friendly, smoothly-functioning operation takes constant effort and dedication, especially when every night has the feel of a Broadway opening.

As the sun begins to sink, the curtain rises at III Forks. The first guests arrive around 5 o'clock. By 6:30 the restaurant is buzzing. Guests mill around the lobby. Drinks flow at the bar. Waiters scurry by. A staff of over 130 employees keeps III Forks going seven evenings a week. As many as

*Dale Wamstad greeting customers at the bar.*
*This kind of personal attention is part of what makes*
*the III Forks dining experience so special.*

140 tables may be occupied on any given night, requiring a staff of 50 wait-ers, 12 bussers, 10 hostesses, 15 expeditors and 8 bartenders.

Not surprising, when you play to virtually a packed house for each per-formance, the reviews are spectacular. John Rizzuti, a local Dallas business-man, points to the personal service. "From Dale down to the wait staff and the people at the front door, I'm always greeted by name. They make you feel special," he told *Eye on Business*, a Dallas/Ft. Worth business journal.

A III Forks regular for both business meetings and social outings, Riz-zuti says, "The food is consistently great. The whole experience is exquisite. I've never dined in a more beautiful restaurant."

One of the heartiest III Forks endorsements comes from CBS television's golf commentator David Feherty who also writes a monthly column for *Golf* magazine. The witty columnist says his road trips for CBS often revolve around the simple pleasure of a good meal.

In his December 2000 column, Feherty wrote, "But the clear winner to me is the Byron Nelson Classic in my hometown of Dallas, Texas, which is also home to the world's greatest steak house, III Forks. Of course a great restaurant is as much about people as it is about food, and Dale Wam-stad is a giant in the business. He founded the leg-endary Del Frisco's before moving on to this latest and greatest venture."

For the beef-loving Feherty, III Forks has his kind of food. "All I want is a nice big steak, which, even though it's cooked all the way through, is tender and juicy; some kind of spud; and plenty of elbow room."

In addition to delivering on the food, III Forks gives Feherty a warm feeling. "Dale and Rick Stein have the ability to make everyone who visits feel special. I thought it was just me, but I've been there enough now to notice otherwise. Also, they've been able to instill the same qualities into his staff, which I think is the real trick. Rick Stein is the epitome of the per-fect front-of-the-house man."

At III Forks, going the extra mile for customers comes from feeling like part of the team. That bond was formed months before the restaurant

# There's No Place Like III Forks

Dave Burns loves to eat out. "I've sat down to dinner in 41 states and view the invention of 'going out to eat' as one of the great strides forward in civilization," notes the Florida businessman. But nothing in his dining experience compares with III Forks.

"If you visit the Dallas-Fort Worth area and don't go to III Forks, you've shot yourself in the hoof," he adds. "Dale Wamstad has created an experience that most closely resembles being an honored guest in a friend's home."

A III Forks veteran, Burns urges visitors to enjoy the restaurant memorabilia associated with early Texas history. You should also say 'hi' to General Manager Rick Stein ("One of the best people on the planet. He takes a personal interest in everything and everyone at III Forks, especially you.").

"Of course you're there for the food," Burns reminds you. "As befits a great steak house, the menu is decidedly American with outstanding steaks and chops."

But, according to Burns, some unexpected and delicious surprises await you when you sit down at this restaurant. Among these, he lists the apples in the house salad and some of the best crabcakes anywhere. But he cautions patrons to save room for dessert, "including terrific ice cream that's made right here," he says.

opened when Wamstad hired many of his key employees and put them to work sanding floors, staining railings, putting up crown molding, and painting walls.

Ask Stein about those pre-opening months, and he'll mention cleanliness. "Dale runs the cleanest construction site you can imagine, just like his restaurant."

Once, after a day of construction and sweeping up electrical snippets, Stein approached Wamstad, "You're paying me a lot of money, shouldn't I be writing a manual or planning the restaurant opening?"

Wamstad threw his arm around his genial general manager-to-be, saying, "I want you to feel like you built this place and own it."

Each of those early employees has memories of those pre-opening days. Connie Trujillo, a jack-of-all-trades in the kitchen (and really second in command), remembers staining the walls. Chris Vogeli became a virtual construction assistant, helping to paint and working daily with the staff at the site. Motivation was a key and "Dale fired us up with his vision," Vogeli recalls.

Adds Landgraf, "The fact that so many employees have been with him for so long says a lot about Dale and the way he does things. And then there are the customers who come here because they'd eaten in his other restaurants, and love Dale."

According to Wamstad, "We try to create an experience. I want guests to leave here feeling they got their money's worth."

Likening his management style to that of famed World War II General George Patton, Wamstad insists that the III Forks staff do it his way. "It may not be the right thing in your eyes, but through my experience I've found out that this is the way it should be done."

A demanding employer, Wamstad is tough but tender. Just ask Connie Trujillo, who came into Texas from Mexico years ago, carrying her little boy across the Rio Grande. She started with Wamstad in 1990 at Del Frisco's and is now one of the backbones of the staff. She has a smile that lights up every corner of the kitchen where she's working.

A stunning oil painting of Connie hangs outside the kitchen next to the Oyster Bar. "A week after we opened, Dale was yelling my name." Connie was thinking "Uh-oh, what did I do wrong."

She came to the front of the kitchen where all the staff had gathered. When Dale unveiled the picture of her, she wept. "Oh, it was so emotional," she said, her voice choking up even now, years after that moment.

*Connie Trujillo is one of the integral components
of the III Forks team, overseeing much of the
preparation in the restaurant's kitchen*

"When people I used to work with come to eat, they say, 'Tierney, you look so much happier.' And it's true because I love this place."

"Dale is like my second daddy, and I have a dream job," she adds, echoing the sentiment of more III Forks staffers than one can count.

One of those is Office Manager Tierney Jory. "When people I used to work with come to eat, they say, 'Tierney, you look so much happier.' And it's true because I love this place."

On a bright early winter morning, Jory is bringing a coffee pot to the table where Wamstad sits, dressed casually but neatly in a western shirt and khakis with brown, well-worn cowboy boots.

It's 10 A.M., and all is quiet at III Forks. It's also spotless because no staff member leaves the restaurant at night until every table is reset, every plate is cleaned and put away, and every nook and cranny of the kitchen is dirt-, dust-, and crumb-free. "In the morning when I open up, one of my tasks is to re-inspect everything for cleanliness," Jory adds.

The main dining room—the Lafayette Room—is spacious and filled with light. Near the bar, an employee is buffing the floor. Occasionally a phone rings in the office where two employees handle reservations. It's peaceful at III Forks, but this is only temporary.

*Tierney Jory plays piano for diners
in the upstairs Promenade Room*

## III Forks

CHAPTER TWO

# A DREAM BECOMES REALITY

W hat I like about Dale is that he isn't just a dreamer, he makes his dreams happen," says Lisa Webb, the Assistant Banquet Manager at III Forks. "Way back when I worked for him at Del Frisco's, he talked about a restaurant like III Forks, and he wasn't afraid to make it happen."

When he thought of III Forks, Wamstad says, "I thought about creating a great place where everybody could come for dinner, banquets, parties, and weddings. Something that was more than a steak house, that also did great seafood and lamb chops."

Today, when he walks through the front door of this grand establishment, what does Wamstad feel?

"A great sense of pride. It was my dream. I built it. I'm living it," he says, sweeping his arm around the dining room. "Everything you see is handcrafted and original, from the woodwork to the mirrors, from the chandeliers to the murals. The decor popped out of my head as did other things like the gold bread bowls with deer antlers."

Best known in restaurant circles as the originator of Del Frisco's Steak House, Wamstad was born in Spokane, Washington. His father was a Norwegian from Iowa and his mother was Irish from Spokane. When Wamstad was 12, the family moved to New Orleans when his Dad was transferred there.

Although it would take him decades to find his restaurant groove, Wamstad recalls, "I fell in love with New Orleans cooking."

He started selling insurance when he was 21 and followed the money to nicer neighborhoods and better homes. "I wasn't the smartest agent, but I'd be in the office by eight every morning and work long hours."

Wamstad did well and in 1976 joined a group that purchased a Popeye's fried chicken franchise in Louisville, Kentucky. He was still selling insurance but the foodservice business fascinated him.

"All of a sudden I'm in an industry where you do everything right and people walk through your door and buy your products," he says, noting the stark contrast with the "make-a-dozen-calls, get-a-lead" drill of selling insurance.

A big believer in Popeye's, Wamstad still loves their product, but the economy in the mid-1970s was against the group. "We grew too fast, one thing led to another and Popeye's failed in Louisville."

Wamstad ended up broke but still intrigued by the restaurant industry. If he was going to get into the business, why not take the high road— an upscale steak house.

"I'd spent so much time in Popeye's that my insurance business had eroded. So I had a choice: go back into insurance, which I absolutely hated, or go into a business I knew nothing about, but that I loved."

Following his heart, Wamstad roamed the country looking for his first steakhouse. On business in Louisville one day, he spotted a local newspaper ad announcing that a restaurant was for lease off of Shelbyville Road.

Negotiations moved swiftly, and the owner, anxious to retire, leased the restaurant and everything in it to Wamstad for $2,000 a month. Suddenly the insurance salesman was a full-fledged restaurateur with no idea what he was doing. The name Del Frisco's derived from Wamstad's given name of Dale Francis.

Charlie Weeks, an attorney from Jackson, Mississippi, and a friend who goes way back with Dale, was a partner in that first Del Frisco's in Louisville.

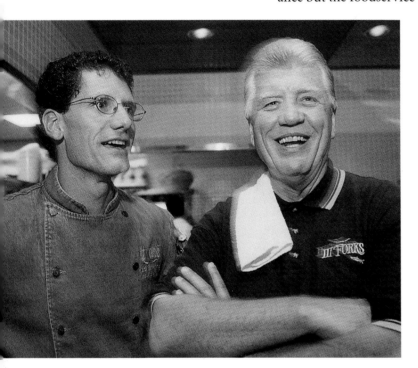

■

*ABOVE: Wamstad and Executive Chef Chris Vogeli share a laugh in the kitchen*

*RIGHT: Dale Wamstad, the visionary behind III Forks*

"I first met Dale when he was in the life insurance business, and I've been with him for a long time. He's a workaholic and definitely has the touch of success with his restaurants. He gets results."

With that first Del Frisco's, Wamstad and his partners sold out for $50,000 to a group from Denver. Wamstad got to retain the Del Frisco's name everywhere but within a 50-mile radius of Louisville. So he headed home to New Orleans and opened Del Frisco's in Gretna, a suburb of New Orleans on the West Bank of the Mississippi River.

The move to New Orleans prompted a crisis in the kitchen but proved to be a turning point in Wamstad's restaurant career.

When his chef from Louisville asked for too much money to be the chef in New Orleans, Wamstad went to work in the kitchen, the first time he'd been there regularly since he was a part-time butcher when he was 19.

"Not keeping that chef was the best thing that happened to me," he recalls. "It put me in the kitchen for the next 14 years. I cut the meat, trimmed the tenderloins, did all the prep work—everything from A to Z. I never left the kitchen through all my years with Del Frisco's."

From 1982 to 1989, Wamstad opened other Del Frisco's. Then in 1985 he launched one in Dallas, bringing a number of his employees from the New Orleans restaurant with him to prepare the new place. Among these was a cute, dark-haired lady named Colleen Keating, who was 21 years his junior.

Like the pre-opening labor at III Forks more than a decade later, Wamstad had some key employees working on the new Del Frisco's before its opening in Dallas. That's how he and Colleen got together. Here's his version: "One evening I took this little gal, covered head to foot from staining and sanding, and said 'Come on, I'll buy you a hamburger.' So every night, I said 'Come on I'll buy you a hamburger.' One thing led to another and we were mar-

*Wamstad occasionally stops into the kitchen to give Kitchen Manager Asif Raza a refresher on the best way to cut a steak*

ried in 1987. Now we have the three most beautiful children you've ever seen."

Colleen says, "He asked me out to this dumpy little drive-in place with a lofty name—Prince of Hamburgers. The rest is history. Today we have a 13-year-old girl, Dale Frances Wamstad. Dale calls her E. Then there's our boy, Dane, who's 11 and Shelby Rose is 9."

One of Wamstad's friends is Houston Oppenheimer, a Louisville attorney. The two men first met when Oppenheimer represented Wamstad and his group as they developed their Popeye's franchise. Since then, Oppenheimer has been with Wamstad through good times and bad, including a period in the mid-1980s when the restaurateur didn't "have two nickels to rub together."

Although they're good friends, Oppenheimer and Wamstad have dramatically different styles. "I'm an attorney and rather conservative," Oppenheimer notes. "He's a free-spirited entrepreneur who's willing to put it all on the line."

That was evident with the development of Del Frisco's on Spring Valley Road in Dallas.

"Dale fell in love with this property on Spring Valley Road," Oppenheimer recalls. "He wanted Colleen to own the real estate and he would own the business, so he developed a Del Frisco's there. It was somewhere between 6,000 and 7,000 square feet with a copper roof and a cupola."

At the time, Wamstad was involved with a Del Frisco's in Addison, Texas and another on Lemmon Avenue. But his heart was on Spring Valley Road.

"Del Frisco's in Addison had parking problems, and the Del Frisco's on Lemmon Avenue had environmental problems," Oppenheimer recalls. "In May of 1993 both steak houses closed down. Then on June 3, 1993 Del Frisco's opened on Spring Valley Road and became one of the most successful steak houses in America."

In 1995, Del Frisco's on Spring Valley Road booming, Wamstad sold it for a stunning $23 million to Jamie Coul-

*Dale Wamstad dines in one of III Forks' intimate upstairs-dining rooms along with his wife, Colleen, family, and friends*

# As III Forks rose from the ground, Colleen kept saying "It's getting too big, you could do the Virginia reel through here."

ter of Lone Star Steakhouse and Saloon. "Man, it was just too strong an offer to resist," Wamstad says.

After working briefly with Lone Star as a consultant, the company and Wamstad parted ways. Oppenheimer, who represented his friend at the sale, explains that, "They came to a mutual decision that he was too entrepreneurial."

Looking back on the Lone Star deal, Oppenheimer says, "It was, and still may be, the largest sale price in America for a single restaurant."

In 1995, at age 54 and still full of vigor, Wamstad was out of the restaurant business. "But how do you retire your mind? For six months you might lay around, but I had ideas."

That same year he spotted a piece of property in North Dallas that was known in the early 1800s as the III Forks Territory. In Texas lore this territory was a boisterous wild west town where drovers assembled for the long and dangerous Chisolm Trail ride from Texas to Dodge City, Kansas. As the story goes, it was also the scene of many battles involving the fiercely independent cattlemen of the day. Wamstad likes to say that III Forks was founded in 1838 and re-opened in 1998 when III Forks restaurant opened.

"I always had plans for a III Forks in this area," he explains. "I thought of putting a restaurant here, but not one of this magnitude. It took two-and-a-half years to build. Heck, it just developed and became more and more. I'll always be proud of Del Frisco's, but I'm a little partial to this child right now."

When the Del Frisco's sale to Lone Star was brewing, Colleen had urged her husband not to sell. "I knew he'd regret it. You can't build something all those years and not have withdrawal pains. But he sold it anyway; he never listens to me."

Colleen says, the Del Frisco's on Spring Valley Road was originally going to be III Forks. "It's been on his mind a long time. He's always wanted to do this place in Dallas where you could go and have weddings and that

# John Harkey Makes It Happen at CRC

As John Harkey and John Cracken were building their hugely successful private-equity firm, Cracken, Harkey & Co., L.L.C., in the 1990s, the word on the street was that the restaurant industry was perceived as out of favor and should be avoided, Harkey recalls.

Not heeding that advice, Harkey has in recent years consolidated seven restaurant operations into Consolidated Restaurant Companies, Inc. (CRC), a restaurant holding company which operates and franchises 157 restaurants and generates over $200 million a year in annual revenues. Today CRC is the 36th largest private company in North Texas.

A consummate businessman, Harkey compares the restaurant industry to a manufacturing process, but with a difference: "In the restaurant business you go from raw ingredient to finished product to the customer consuming the product all in the span of about an hour."

That compressed time frame, plus the volume of meals and instant customer feedback, puts a huge demand on the restaurant operating team to provide superior customer service and products. "We'll feed 25 million people this year," he says with pride.

With those demands on the staff in mind, Harkey believes the key to CRC's success "is our ability to develop an infrastructure that provides the right services to allow our management teams to execute their plans."

A classic example is III Forks. "Dale Wamstad suggested that CRC acquire his operations because he wanted the ability to focus on the creative side of the business while still having some operating involvement," Harkey notes.

CRC bought the real estate including two buildings from Wamstad—the 25,000 square foot III Forks facility and the 8,500 square foot Buttermilk restaurant, which has since ben converted into retail space.

"Dale is now a partner with us, and III Forks fits perfectly with our company," he adds.

CRC has four segments: Italian with Spaghetti Warehouse Restaurants as the flagship; Mexican with El Chico Restaurants leading the way; American Grill with Good Eats Restaurants; and a Social Gathering segment that includes III Forks, Cool River Restaurants and the Silver Fox Restaurant.

"We enjoy working with Dale," Harkey explains. "He's one of the premier steak men in the country, and he continues to run his restaurant."

But there's a crucial difference these days at III Forks. "What was once an operation totally dependent on one person (Wamstad) is now part of a team," Harkey explains. "All the same employees remain, and they operate autonomously, but instead of being burdened by things like in-house accounting or human resources, we handle the back office operations. They can focus on what they're great at, which is satisfying customers."

CRC also brings tremendous economic efficiencies to III Forks and its other restaurants. "III Forks is one restaurant, and we buy 50 times the volume so there are great efficiencies," he adds.

Restaurants were nowhere on Harkey's radar screen while he was at the University of Texas in Austin earning a BBA in Finance with Honors in 1983 and a J.D. in 1986. A year later he added an MBA from Stanford University School of Business.

Although he wasn't a restaurant man, Harkey grew up in the same town of Brownwood, Texas as Gene Street, who is 20 years his senior and one the country's legendary casual-dining restaurateurs.

Harkey is Manager of Cracken, Harkey, Street & Hartnett, L.L.C. (CHSH), a private investment firm, which selectively invests in and acquires full-service casual dining and quick-service restaurant companies.

Harkey spends nearly all his time on restaurant business, formulating and implementing CRC's strategic financial objectives, identifying CHSH's strategic targets, structuring and negotiating the debt financing required to close CHSH's acquisitions, and representing both CHSH and CRC in public and private capital markets.

The back-of-house operating functions for all of CRC's restaurants are handled by Consolidated Restaurant Operations, CRC's operating company, under the direction of Chief Executive Officer Wally Jones.

"Wally and I talk several times a day as do Gene and I," adds Harkey. "We've got tremendous depth and experience on our team with many dedicated enthusiastic people who love the restaurant business."

"I had heard of Gene, and our families knew each other," Harkey recalls. "I was looking at an industry to invest in and found El Chico. He heard about it, called me and said, 'Are you trying to buy El Chico?' I said 'I might be.' He said, 'Let's partner.'"

The two men teamed up in the fall of 1997 and CRC purchased El Chico in January 1998. In addition to serving as Chairman of the Board of CRC,

As for III Forks, Harkey says he gets a tremendous kick watching customers enjoy the restaurant and hearing compliments of the staff. "The professionalism of the entire team is extraordinary," he says. "It's great to be associated with a truly unique steak house."

sort of thing. On the original drawings for Del Frisco's on Spring Valley Road, it says III Forks."

As III Forks rose from the ground, Colleen kept saying "It's getting too big, you could do the Virginia reel through here."

Looking back, she says he was right about the size. "There was a need for a place like this. It's big and warm. Businesses can come in and have meetings and not get food at 7 P.M. that was cooked at 12 noon. It's good to get a steak cut to order, nice and fresh."

Although he's never regretted leaving the insurance business, Wamstad has applied lessons learned from those days to building his restaurant clientele.

"The toughest job in the world is selling life insurance because you're selling an intangible that people can't see," he explains. "I just took the techniques from those days of writing thank you notes and appreciating your customers and applied them to restaurants."

Night after night, after Del Frisco's closed for the evening, Wamstad would sit hunched over his desk, often until three in the morning, penning notes to customers who had visited that evening. He'd also send birthday greetings, congratulatory notes, and Christmas cards to friends and people he'd recently met.

With a disdain for technology that continues to this day, he would write every note by hand, often consulting a three-ring binder jammed with names, addresses, and business cards.

"You have to force yourself to do it, and they have to be handwritten. Plus, you can't let it build up," Wamstad notes, recalling that he averaged 10 thank you notes a day, 300 a month, 3,600 a year—a grinding, highly disciplined effort that paid off over the years.

"The best customers you have are existing customers and referrals," he points out. "You develop real relationships with them. I can't tell you how many customers come into this place and say, 'You know, Dale, I've still

*John Harkey, Dale Wamstad, and Gene Street:
the driving force behind III Forks' success*

# Gene Street Turns to Fine Dining

One of the Southwest's best known casual-dining operators and the acknowledged "King of Chicken Fried Steak," Gene Street is finding life a little different on the fine dining side.

After creating the famed Black Eyed Pea chain, the Dixie House chain, and dozens of other restaurant concepts, Street is now chairman of Consolidated Restaurant Operations (CRO), the operating company of Consolidated Restaurant Companies, Inc., which owns El Chico Restaurants, Spaghetti Warehouse, the Good Eats Grill chain, Cool River Restaurants in Austin, Dallas, and Denver, and a host of other successful stand-alone concepts.

"I came up in the restaurant industry through casual dining where it's 'turn those tables, turn those tables,'" says Street, as personable an executive as you'll find in the restaurant industry. He is also highly acclaimed, with dozens of awards to his credit. These include Restaurateur of the Year by the Texas Restaurant Association, and a coveted High Impact Leadership Award from *Restaurants & Business* magazine.

When Street and his partners at Consolidated—John Harkey, Steve Hartnett and John Cracken—acquired III Forks, it was a big step into a new area for the veteran restaurateur.

"At III Forks, when guests come in, they come for an experience. They come to soak up all the glamour and glitter of this place. They want to be waited on and pampered," says Street of III Forks' customers, who routinely linger at their tables for up to two hours.

That change of pace has been a real education for Street. "I put my feet in the guest's shoes and remember when I went to a fine restaurant before III Forks. It's a different world. The evening is going to hold special memories for those people."

Obviously he's made the adjustment. "Gene Street is a prince," says General Manager Rick Stein. "He's an incredible operator. When he came into this restaurant as a patron, he always made it a point to know my name, and that was long before he was ever interested in becoming involved with III Forks."

Like many others, what drew Street to III Forks was Dale Wamstad. "For 15 years I've been an admirer and competitor of his. With Dale you always know where you stand. He's the most quality, by-the-books guy I've ever met."

The Consolidated/III Forks deal began when Wamstad called Street and said, "Let's get together." Not long afterwards, the two restaurateurs, joined by Harkey, met and hammered out a deal.

"Our vision meshed with Dale's, and he wanted to kick back a little," Street recalls. "But he's still at III Forks almost every night working the dining room. He might take off Sundays now, but I've never seen anyone work a room like Dale. With his unique voice, silver hair, and six-foot-three-inch frame, he's an imposing figure."

Then in his typically candid fashion, Street adds, "I tell you, he's a tough act to follow."

Consolidated Restaurant Operations provides III Forks with strong support in back-of-the-house purchasing, human resources, and accounting. "These were all the details that used to take up so much of Dale's time," Street explains.

According to Street, " The first thing you notice at III Forks is the professionalism —how sharp everyone looks, how everything is done just right. Dale makes sure of that. They have an exceptional staff there, and our company is proud to be involved with these people."

The fact that III Forks lives up to its rave reviews on a nightly basis makes it a prime location for corporate events. "We do an incredible number of private parties and functions—ranging from 10 to 350 people—for medical companies, drug firms, civic organizations, and high-tech groups," observes Street.

III Forks also gives back to the community. Blessed with good fortune from the day its doors opened in 1998, the restaurant hosts a major charity event or benefit free of charge every month in its Courtyard area.

"People submit proposals," explains Street. "These could be for a school, a children's cause or a medical benefit, but we're very strong on giving back to the community."

got a thank you letter you sent me in 1989. It's posted on my wall.'"

Those letters, and word of mouth, used to be all Wamstad did in the way of promotion. He remembered that in New Orleans in the 1980's restaurants never advertised. " If you advertised, it meant you weren't any good and people wouldn't come, so all the great restaurants in New Orleans refused to advertise."

He's done a 180 degree turnaround. "In the late 1980s, the business climate changed with more competition coming in and the oil industry going down."

His marketing efforts, like most Wamstad ventures, are big, bold, and very different. For example, his radio spots for III Forks are folksy, almost corny, and not highly regarded from a creative standpoint by the advertising community.

Wamstad says a typical spot might begin, " 'This is the big dog of III Forks, the crown jewel of American dining' . . . and then I'd just rap on and on. These commercials definitely got the attention of people driving home at night."

Says Dallas restaurateur Gene Street, "Listening to those radio ads makes people want to come to III Forks and meet Dale Wamstad."

Restaurateurs like Wamstad typically have a tough time carving room in their busy lives to spend with family. Mindful of this, Wamstad and his wife have worked hard to keep a balance.

"Even in my years with Del Frisco's, Colleen would drop by at 5 or 5:30 in the afternoon so I could visit with the kids," he says. " The quality time has always been there, and the main force behind that is Colleen."

"We made sure he saw the kids," Colleen says. "I'd either drive them up there to say 'hi' or he'd pop home."

When Wamstad gets on the subject of family, he includes his staff. Asif Raza has been with him 17 years; Connie Trujillo, 11 years; Rick Stein, eight years; and Leslie

*Wamstad making his way through the dining room. Every party is personally greeted by at least one member of the management team during their visit to III Forks.*

*General Manager Rick Stein*
*greets patrons at the main entrance*

Vogeli, 12 years. In addition, Chris Vogeli, Steve Tufts, Lisa Webb, and many others have been hard-working and loyal employees with Wamstad since the Del Frisco's days.

"These are people I'd die for," he says with passion. "They're more than employees. But they also know when they disappoint me. All I have to do is look at them and they know. But they do very well and deserve the money and benefits."

But as III Forks flourished, even with a dedicated and smooth-functioning staff, Wamstad found that he couldn't let go. He was keeping the same frantic pace that he established for himself at Del Frisco's.

"I felt I had to be there constantly and oversee everything," he recalls, voicing a familiar lament of independent restaurateurs.

Deciding that a change was needed, he talked with his friend, Gene Street, who had developed the Black Eyed Pea chain and was now chief executive officer of Consolidated Restaurant Company, Inc.

"I told Gene, 'What if I sell to you all, and we work together," Wamstad explains. That sounded good to Street who immediately called his partner, John Harkey, chairman of Consolidated Restaurant Company, Inc. The two men then met with Wamstad and struck a deal.

"I'm still the proprietor and everyone works for me, but I don't have the burden of being the sole guy," he adds. "Put another way, I'm still the jerk and still want it done right, but I don't spend anywhere near the time I used to spend here."

Warren Leruth, himself a noted chef and former restaurateur in New Orleans, thinks Wamstad made a smart decision because the restaurant business is tough on people. "He's a great operator, but every year you spend in this business is like three or four years in another business. That's because you're always dealing with things like labor, customers, and making sure things are done right all the time."

# "I'm still the proprietor and everyone works for me, but I don't have the burden of being the sole guy…"

Despite the cutback in hours, Wamstad is still very much at the helm of III Forks. "He's done a lot for the restaurant industry in this town," adds Colleen. "He's not easy because he demands perfection, but the end result is that the customer is happy."

In a view that Wamstad shares, Colleen adds, "If you're trying to get something for nothing, don't come to III Forks. A lot of places don't want to make anyone angry, so customers who complain when nothing's wrong can get away with it, but not here."

"And you know what?" she says. "I think the employees, especially the waitstaff, appreciate that. They know that no one is going to push them around if they're doing their job."

*Executive Chef Chris Vogeli, Kitchen Manager Asif Raza, and Assistant Chef Gregory Moreaux form the kitchen front line for the evening's preparations.*

## III Forks

### CHAPTER THREE

# IT'S SHOW TIME

Executive Chef Chris Vogeli has his kitchen routine down pat. Just before the restaurant opens at 5 P.M., he calls his staff together for a line check and to discuss the evening ahead.

"I taste every sauce, check the soups and seasonings, and examine the first batch of potatoes. I look at all the drawers to make sure beef is there, and the fish is all cut. I make sure the salads, sides, and appetizers are ready. Then," he pauses for effect, "it's show time!"

That means serving steaks, prime beef, lamb chops, and seafood to 500 to 1,000 guests a night.

"We bring in the best ingredients," Vogeli says. "It's all USDA prime beef from the midwest where the cattle are corn fed. We get the most incredible tasting crab meat. It was caught the night before in the Gulf, put on a plane in the morning, and is in our kitchen by four o'clock."

Vogeli's day actually begins around 1 P.M. when he checks with National Director of Sales Pamela Landgraf to see what parties are on tap for the evening. Then he makes a prep list for the staff, including how many tubs of lettuce are needed, how many cases of corn, how many crabcakes, and how many pounds of shrimp.

"When we open for dinner we have eight people back here cleaning tenderloins and cutting steaks to order when the tickets come in," he explains.

Wamstad comes in every evening. "He'll ask how everything is going and did we get the beef order," says Vogeli. The personable 36-year-old chef remembers when III Forks first opened, and no one but Wamstad did the beef order. "I did the fish but he wouldn't let us do the beef."

The first time Wamstad went on vacation, he insisted that Vogeli fax him the beef inventory so he could call in the order. "When he finally passed the beef order duty over to me, I felt like I'd made it, that I'd graduated."

Born and raised in Dallas, Vogeli's parents, Tilly and Werner, are both natives of Switzerland. Werner Vogeli did his cooking apprenticeship in Zurich and spent 27 years as chef of the City Club, a Dallas businessmen's organization. He retired in 1999 but keeps active in cooking by teaching in a culinary program at a local Dallas art institute.

After graduating from high school, Vogeli wanted to check out the computer industry and took a summer job behind a desk. "I realized I was too active for that," says the sports-loving chef, "so I told my father I wanted to be in foodservice."

"You're going to Switzerland and start like I did," Werner Vogeli replied.

After spending a few years attending culinary programs in Dallas and also at the Loews Anatole Hotel (now the Wyndham Anatole) in foodservice, he eventually made it to Switzerland in 1986, starting at the Dolder Grande Hotel in Zurich.

Even with his background in foodservice in Dallas, Vogeli said the European experience was like starting over again. "Over there, they make everything from scratch. In America we worry a lot about labor, food often being secondary. But there it's totally opposite. Food is on a pedestal. It wouldn't matter how much labor you had to use to achieve the right dish."

For example, Vogeli would get ducks in the kitchen with their feathers plucked but nothing else. "We had to cut off the head and feet. In America you typically get ducks and chickens that are frozen."

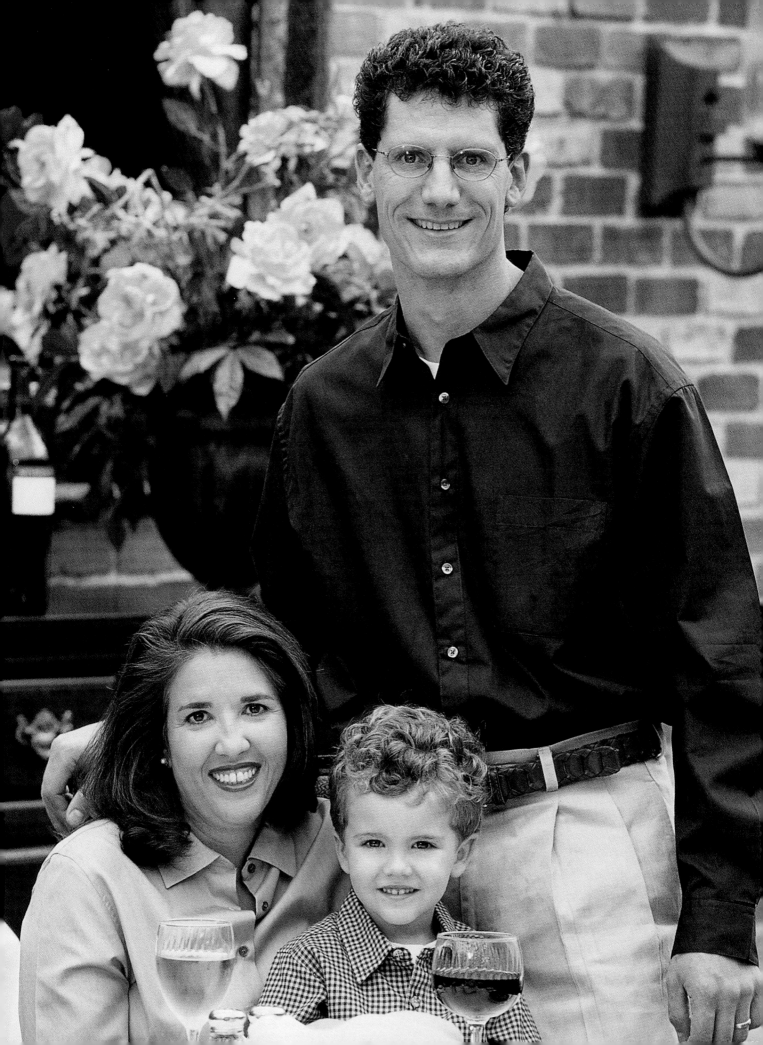

# While Vogeli learned much about his trade in Europe, he hasn't emulated the management style of many of the chefs he met there…

After working in European restaurants until 1989, Vogeli returned to Dallas, eventually spending five years in the service division of the Marriott Corporation working on corporate functions.

He met Wamstad through his wife, Leslie, who had been a waitress, hostess, and then the office manager at Del Frisco's.

While Vogeli learned much about his trade in Europe, he hasn't emulated the management style of many of the chefs he met there.

"I worked with some strict, tyrant chefs in Europe—the classic screamers," he recalls. "I'm more relaxed. I think you get more from people by being fair. We have a strong group here, and once you acquire their trust, they're loyal to you. You don't do that by yelling and screaming."

When he started at III Forks, Vogeli says, "I was strong on sauces, salads, and soups, as well as fish, desserts, and bread. However, I didn't know much about beef and broiling. I learned that from Dale."

At III Forks, a plaque hangs on the wall of the stairway leading to the second floor. It represents one of Vogeli's many culinary achievements:

INTERNATIONAL BANQUET AWARD
THE WORLD MASTER CHEFS SOCIETY
DALLAS 1997

"I was captain of the culinary team that won the cooking competition against teams from all over the world," he proudly explains.

Looking into his kitchen, Vogeli says two words come to mind—fresh and clean.

*ABOVE: Chef Chris Vogeli receiving some pointers from his chef-father Werner*
*LEFT: Vogeli with wife Leslie and son Chase*

*Kitchen Manager Asif Raza cutting
the evenings steak orders*

You hear those words often at III Forks. Seafood arrives daily, including lobster tails from Australia, trout from Idaho, and salmon from the Pacific Northwest.

To borrow a phrase from the wine industry, no entree at III Forks gets cooked before its time. "We don't have microwaves or heat lamps in this kitchen to keep things warm," says Vogeli. "We start cooking when the order comes in."

"Our beef goes from the broiler to your plate. It's the same with vegetables and mashed potatoes. Everything is cooked in small batches throughout the evening to make sure it's fresh."

At night when III Forks is busy—and that's virtually every night of the week—Vogeli serves as the kitchen expeditor and also cuts the meat, while overseeing every plate before it leaves the kitchen. But others can also handle those tasks, including Asif Raza and Connie Trujillo.

Broiling steaks and lamb chops to perfection is crucial at III Forks, and no one does it better than Raza, the restaurant's master broiler.

Born in Pakistan, the 32-year-old Raza has probably broiled more steaks than anybody in Dallas during his 17-year career. He's done so many, in fact, that he goes strictly by sight.

"I have an eye for it. I can look at a steak and know it's done the way a customer orders it," he says with a cheery smile and twinkle of the eye that has made him a favorite both at III Forks and previously at Del Frisco's where he met Wamstad.

Raza came to the United States from Pakistan when he was 9 and started washing dishes at Del Frisco's on Lemmon Avenue when he was 15.

But washing dishes wasn't Raza's greatest skill. "I was the worst dishwasher in the history of any restaurant. I'd have them stacked up to the roof and was behind all the time, even with a dishwashing machine."

Fortunately the Del Frisco's staff saw beyond the dirty

plates to Raza's can-do attitude and shifted him to a side station where he learned to broil steaks.

"Dale trained me and worked with me," he says. "He'd cut the meat and I'd broil it. Just watching how he cut and ran the kitchen made me better. He taught me how to look at a steak and tell if it's tough or to see the marbling (the whitish streaks of inter- and intra-muscular fat, found in muscles, which add to the meat's flavor and tenderness)."

"I love it here. Dale has given me the title of master broiler," he adds, noting that he has also shifted into the role of teacher. "I help the other cooks by showing them how to blister the steaks (seal juices in and add to the color) and how to salt and pepper them and season them properly."

With so much beef being cut and ordered in the kitchen, III Forks puts its six broilers to good use. One of the employees working the broiler every night is Assistant Executive Chef Gregory Moreaux, known as Frenchy.

He's been at III Forks virtually since it opened but took the job only after much thought. "I had a strong background in French restaurants so when I was offered the job, it was my first steak house experience. I took a few days to think about it."

To help with his decision, Frenchy sat at the III Forks Oyster Bar and watched the kitchen in action. He was impressed.

"It looked very good," he explains. "It looked like something that would work for a long time. I love it here. It's very challenging, and the quality and quantity of food we do every night for so many guests just amazes me."

Another factor Frenchy noticed from his Oyster Bar perch as he was pondering his job offer was the cleanliness of the kitchen. "Dale is very big on cleanliness," he notes. "We're always sweeping and mopping the floor. Everything is spotless."

According to Office Manager Tierney Jory, "They inspect for cleanliness at night before closing, and I reinspect in the morning. It pays off. Our pest control guy was here

*Assistant Chef Gregory Moreaux manning
one of the restaurant's six broiler stations*

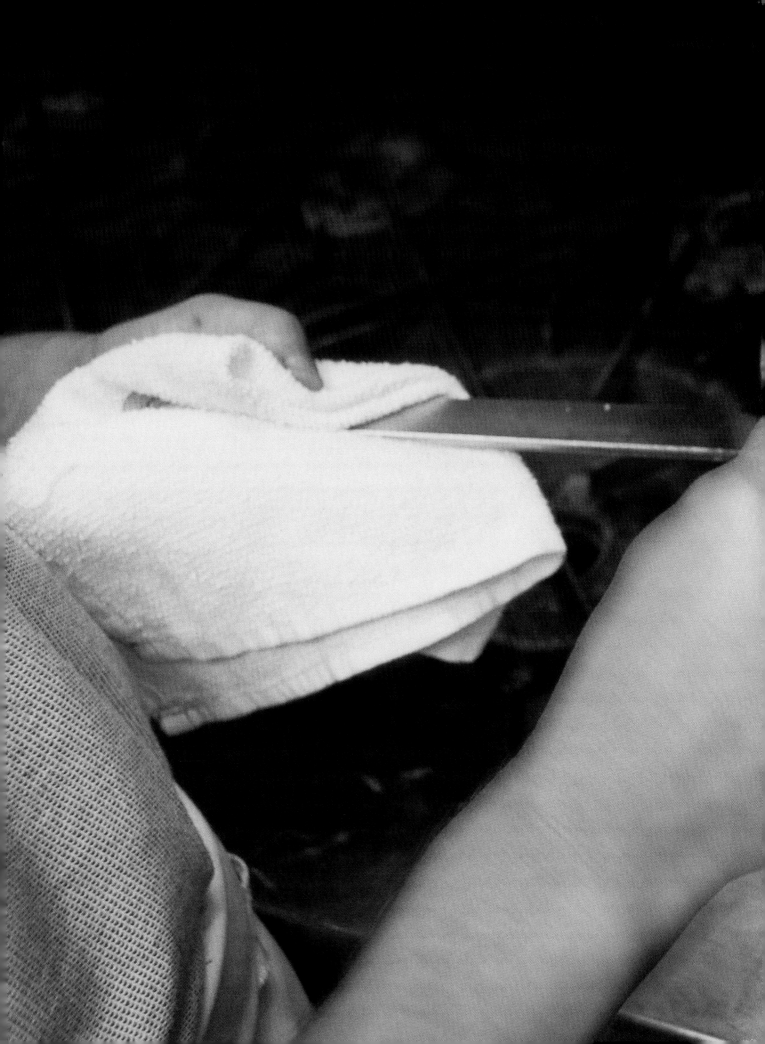

the other day and said, 'This is the cleanest restaurant I've ever seen.'"

A tour of the III Forks kitchen with Wamstad invariably focuses on cleanliness. "Look underneath those drains," he says, pointing to the floor. "It's spotless."

"Gone are the days in foodservice when your restaurant gets dirty and you hold a GI party on Saturday with everyone coming in and scrubbing the place," Wamstad adds. "Cleanliness has to be an every day, every moment thing. When you walk out of here at night, it's clean. And you do that every night."

This focus on cleanliness is perhaps the reason the kitchen at III Forks is so exposed to the public. Anyone seated at the Oyster Bar or walking to the Lafayette Room

*LEFT: Roasting lobster for lobster bisque*
*ABOVE: Preparing fresh greens
for the day's salads*

# That's crucial to the restaurant's success— serving fresh food when the guest is ready.

can look right down the kitchen line where Chris Vogeli or Connie Trujillo is pulling down order slips and cutting beef for the broilers.

"Customers can walk into our kitchen anytime, and it will be clean," Wamstad adds. "I've always been fanatical about this."

Another key to the success of III Forks is its ability to serve fresh "just in time" food—juicy, thick steaks and tender, fresh fish—to very large numbers of people.

"Our ordering system is great," says Steve Tufts, the waiter in charge of the 25-seat Captain's Room, a popular site for business meetings.

When the waitstaff at III Forks delivers the order to the kitchen, it reaches the grill within three or four minutes. But since everything is cooked to order, servers, working closely with the kitchen staff, can pace their orders to the needs of their customers.

In Tufts' view, that's one of the beauties of the ordering system. "If guests are lingering over salads, I can let Chris Vogeli know and he can slow down the cooking time. It's something I have control over."

That's crucial to the restaurant's success—serving fresh food when the guest is ready. "You don't want someone to be sitting there enjoying their salad and all of a sudden—wham, bang—here comes the entrée," Tufts adds with a nod to the kitchen crew. "I've got a lot of faith in those people because they make it work every night for 500 to 1,000 guests."

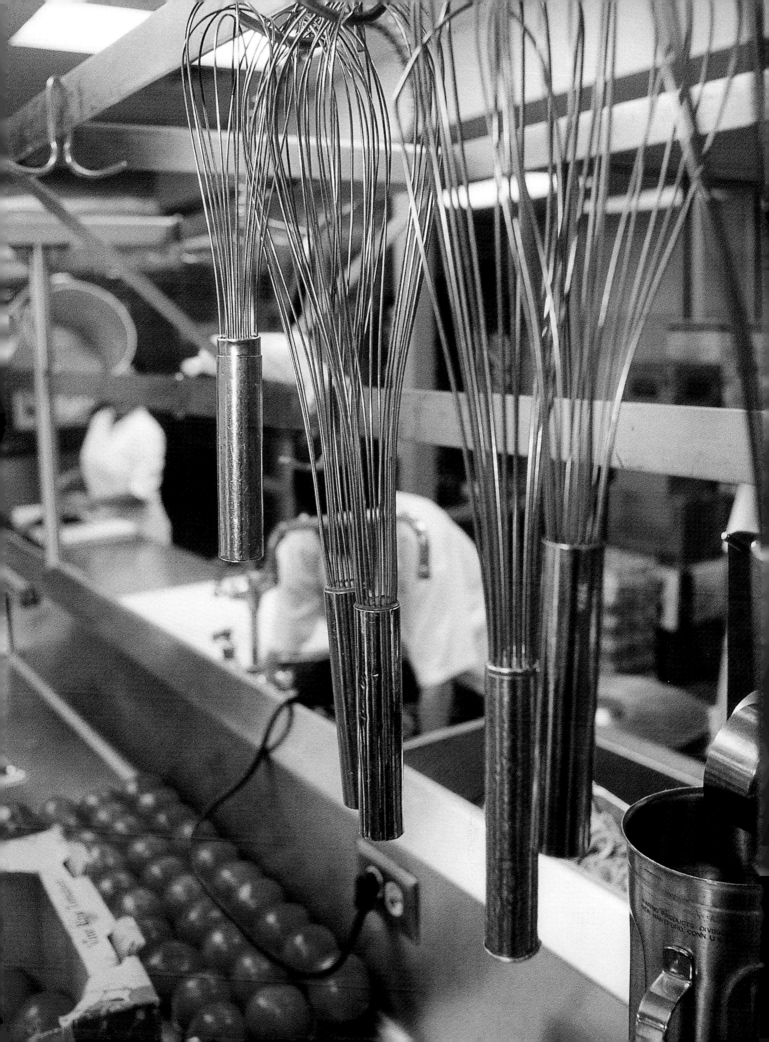

*Diners in the Lafayette Room, with its hand-painted wall murals and unique elk-antler chandeliers*

## III Forks

CHAPTER FOUR

# FINE DINING AT ITS BEST

*Y*es, III Forks is grand, even awesome. It's also warm and inviting. But it wouldn't remain a favorite dinner and meeting venue night after night if it weren't for the food.

From thick signature cuts of USDA prime beef to ocean-fresh fish and buttery lobster, the food at III Forks is perfectly prepared. Everything is fresh, made when you order it. And the wait staff delivers each dish by hand right from the kitchen. No trays at this steak and seafood house.

While many steak houses also offer fish, few provide an equal and mouth-watering balance between fish and beef like III Forks. "Land and sea, beef and fish, side by side," says Wamstad.

That theme is everywhere from the dark green menus with their beef horn and fish icons to the chandeliers with their antler design and clipper ship bow spirits —land and sea, beef and fish.

"Something that separates us from other steak houses is that we serve a great steak and an entire fish menu, including sole, salmon, sea bass, trout and lobster," Wamstad says. "It's something we're proud of."

Houston Oppenheimer, a friend of Wamstad's for 35 years, says, "My favorite is the veal rib chop." However, in Oppenheimer's view, the most astounding decision Wamstad made was to give the customer a full plate of food. "When you go to other top restaurants and get a

# Unbelievable Ice Cream

The ice cream at III Forks is so rich it's hard to believe, and impossible to resist. It's no accident the ice cream tastes so good.

On a trip to Germany three years ago with Colleen and the kids, Wamstad took the family to dinner at a hotel "that had the most fantastic ice cream in the world."

Curious about what set this particular delicacy apart, Wamstad asked foodservice consultant Warren Leruth.

"I learned that it was 19 percent butterfat ice cream, which no one does anymore. Even Ben and Jerry's is only 14 or 15 percent."

Wamstad quickly discovered it wasn't that easy to create 19 percent butterfat ice cream.

III Forks had to purchase a big Emerson ice cream machine, the kind used on military bases in World War II. That was just the start. A blast freezer was also required since the ice cream had to be frozen during its first two days at 30 degrees below freezing so as not to crystallize.

"What at first was going to be a little ice cream machine wound up as a big ice cream machine and a blast freezer."

But there's more. Most dairies today don't make the ice cream base with 19 percent butterfat like they used to. Fortunately, Leruth got the recipe, and Wamstad found a large dairy in Dallas that would do it.

That was the good news. The bad news came when the dairy told Wamstad that the 19 percent recipe would cost twice as much—$9 a gallon instead of $4.50—and that they only did 500 gallons at a time.

"Oh, boy, now I've done it," Wamstad remembers thinking. "But I'd already bought the machine and the freezer so I was locked into buying $4,500 worth of ice cream. But it's been great. People love the ice cream."

ribeye or filet, you get just the piece of meat on a white plate. That doesn't happen at III Forks."

While the III Forks menu is simple, the restaurant offers a feature dish every night, perhaps a different fish or a new way to prepare steak.

A favorite appetizer is Crabcake St. Francis. "The best I've had anywhere," says foodservice consultant Warren Leruth.

Equally impressive are the shrimp. "When I started in the restaurant business with the first Del Frisco's, I used this big shrimp instead of the little ones, because I didn't know any better," says Wamstad, "No one could believe it. People would say, 'You ought to see the shrimp this guy is using.'"

A standout among the soups and salads is the III Forks Salad, noteworthy because the lettuce is tossed with a walnut and molasses vinegar dressing.

"That dressing was made for that salad. It's a perfect fit," says Steve Tufts.

The fish menu ("Fish Market") includes salmon from the Pacific Northwest, trout from Idaho, Dover sole from Dover, and scallops from New England—all of it fresh and cooked to perfection. "We also purchase Australian cold water lobster tails that are the best in the world," Wamstad exclaims.

"It's very, very good food," adds Leruth. "They make everything themselves. Like fresh bread. You don't make it fresh because it's cheaper, you make it that way because the bread will be fresher, and you have total control over your quality."

Leruth calls Wamstad a "perfectionist" when it comes to the food. "That's why he makes his own ice cream, his own desserts, and cuts meats to order. He doesn't believe in frozen. He's all quality."

During the afternoon hours at III Forks, the kitchen comes alive with activity as over 300 ears of corn are shucked and the kernels skimmed into bowls, and more than 400 fresh, ripe tomatoes are sliced and readied.

# 7,000 Bottles and Counting

Kyle Kepner is the III Forks cellar master, responsible for one of the largest wine cellars in Texas with over 7,000 bottles.

The 30-year-old Kepner began as a waiter at III Forks and was promoted to wine steward in 1999. "I learned quickly because in order to make a living here, you have to know how to serve wine."

Early in his III Forks career, Kepner got to know the two men who ran the wine department before him. He was essentially a stockboy who immersed himself in wine, stacking every bottle that came in, asking questions, and going to wine tastings.

He learned well, and today also serves as a floor manager in two of the restaurant's dining rooms, as well as backing up Rick Stein on the general manager's days off.

On the floor, Kepner expertly employs his knowledge of wine. "That's my forte, and with our regulars, we work hard to know what wines they like and the cigars they smoke. We also put them on our VIP list and invite them to wine tastings."

III Forks has more than 5,000 bottles in its wine cellar on the first floor and over a thousand more in the wine wall across from the Austin Room. Although III Forks carries 600 selections, Kepner would love more storage space.

"Almost every table orders a bottle of wine. The right wine with the right food is very, very complimentary," says Kepner whose philosophy is "What works is what you want. We sell about 90 percent red and 10 percent white."

The restaurant also has a half bottle list, and Kepner encourages the waitstaff to sell half bottles of white wines for salads or appetizers and then move to reds.

His own preference includes heavy Cabernets from California. "They compliment steaks really well."

At age 30, Kepner knows he's young to have so much wine responsibility. He's working on his Master's in Wine Certification, a five-year program that few complete. "There are only about 500 of these individuals in the world, and I'm still about 10 years younger than most people who achieve it."

In May 2001 Kepner became a wine sommelier, which is French for "Keeper of the Sleeping Bottles."

One of Kepner's pleasures is when guests ask him to make their wine selections. He also enjoys encouraging diners who regularly drink the same wine to try something different.

Wine is a big part of the III Forks experience—as many as 400 bottles served a night. "It simply enhances everything," Kepner says. "The crispness of white wine matches the salads and appetizers perfectly, while the heavy red brings out the marbling in the steaks, making the meat more flavorful."

But wine selection at III Forks doesn't stop at salads, appetizers, and entrees. "Something else we do really well here," explains the cellar master, "is dessert wine. They're not big sellers across the country, but we sell about 15 to 20 glasses of port each night. We have a 130-year old Madeira by the glass and five dessert wine selections."

A wine enthusiast through and through, Kepner loves his job and is continually poring over wine magazines and journals. "Dale's a lot like my grandfather who died a couple of years ago—a strong, charismatic, imposing man. And he takes care of his staff."

*Wine Steward Kyle Kepner and
Assistant Manager Launa Wilkerson
remove selections from the
restaurant's wine wall*

# $35,000? I'll Take It!

One of the more intriguing wine stories at III Forks comes from Rick Stein, the general manager. "It was last December, and we had one of our wines listed at $35,000 a bottle. We never really wanted to sell it, just have it on the wine list."

When someone would ask Stein for a wine recommendation, he would often jokingly point to the $35,000 bottle. "This is great. I recommend it."

On that December night, one of the III Forks regulars came in, and Stein presented his $35,000 wine. But instead of laughing, this guest said, "I'll take it."

"I thought he was joking," recalls Stein. "But no, he said, 'Bring the bottle here.'"

Still thinking it was a joke, Stein produced the vaulted wine and set it on the table. The guest asked him to open it. Stein did. The guest took a sniff: "It's no good, send it back."

"Maybe I should let it breathe?" asked a horrified Stein. "No, no," came the reply. "It's no good. Get it out of here."

Wamstad, who happened to be close by, came to the table and told Stein to taste the wine. "I did, and it didn't taste good. So Dale said, 'Take it back.'"

Stein took it back and brought another bottle for the customer. But the story got out when a local Fox television news crew came by and put Stein on camera to relate the episode. Since it was December 21, the United Press and Associated Press news services, as well as the BBC and CNN, picked it up, sending this entertaining holiday anecdote worldwide via print and television.

"We got a lot of good press and still have the bottle on display in our cabinet across from the bar," says Stein of his three-and-a-half minutes of fame. "People remember the story and ask about it, and the gentleman who rejected it still comes in two or three times a week."

# Everyone in the kitchen crew is a strong adherent to Wamstad's philosophy of quality at all cost.

"There are no short cuts," says Executive Chef Vogeli. "For example, we have one person making mashed potatoes all night long. They're called duchess potatoes, and we serve them with our brown gravy."

Everyone in the kitchen crew is a strong adherent to Wamstad's philosophy of quality at all cost. That starts with the vendors. "He drives a hard bargain with our purveyors," says Gene Street. "They know not to send a case of tomatoes that isn't perfect. They know not to send unripe corn. Hey, it's hard to get ripe, perfect corn on the cob 365 days a year, but somehow they manage to find it."

As for the beef, Street adds that, "The guys who pack our beef hand inspect every box. Dale has been with them for 15 years, so we get the prime of the prime."

The food at III Forks is so exceptional that Wamstad insists his wait-staff stick to the menu.

"Dale is always telling me to be strong on the floor," says Tufts. "Invariably you'll have guests who come in and want to redo plates their own special ways. But Dale believes in his menu and serves a great product."

Gene Street sees that dedication every night at III Forks. One of Dallas' best-known restaurateurs, Street knows the business. "Believe me, every item that comes out of that kitchen has got to be a masterpiece. For me, it's the steak. I always order it. We also sell a lot of the III Forks Salad."

A typical night at III Forks is a little like traveling around the world. "Last night we had all these people in from Britain, Japan, and Germany," Street adds, his voice rising with enthusiasm. "They had read and heard about III Forks, and we just had a fabulous Monday night."

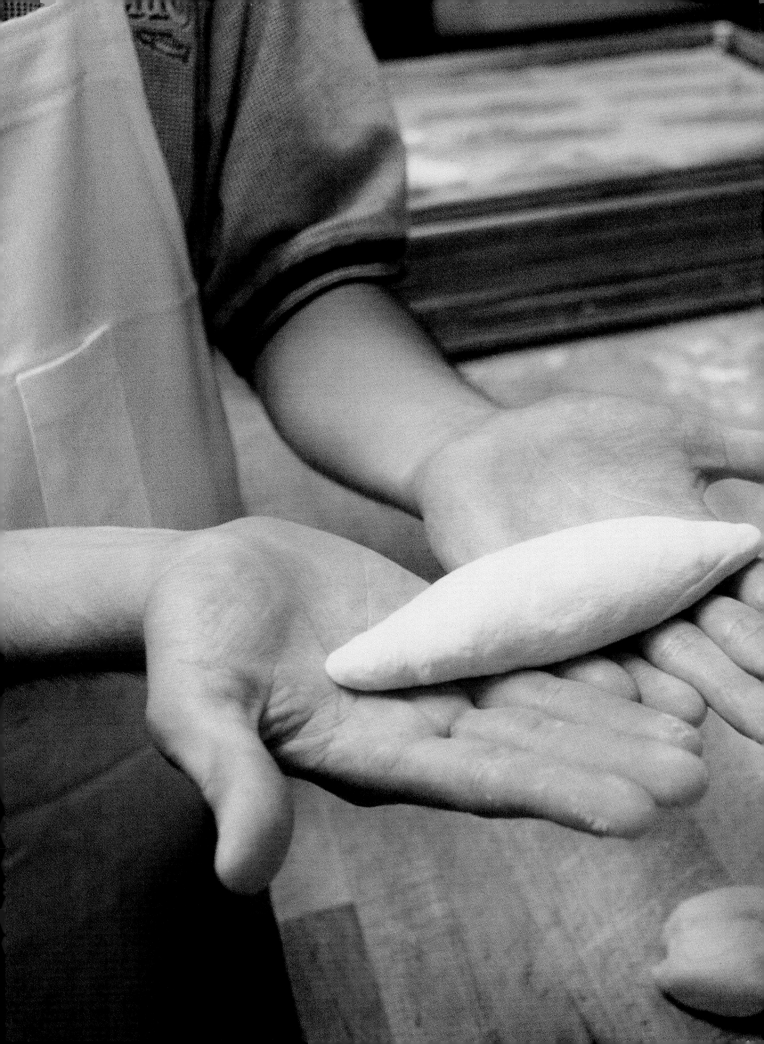

# Bread from Scratch

III Forks makes its own bread every day. Each loaf arrives at your table wrapped in white linen and served in a distinctive brass bowl with deer antlers. The bread is light, warm, and absolutely delicious, which explains why loaf after loaf disappears.

Growing up in New Orleans and then operating a Del Frisco's in Gretna, Wamstad came to love the bread. "People really know how to make it there. Our bread is a take-off of what they call a *pisitelee*—a small French loaf."

Starting at one o'clock everyday, the kitchen crew begins to make the bread, approximately 900 loaves a night. Holding up a piece of the bread, Wamstad says, "This is what I ate growing up in New Orleans."

*Executive Chef Chris Vogeli and
General Manager Rick Stein in front
of the entrance to III Forks*

## III Forks

CHAPTER FIVE

# TIME FOR A TOUR

Like all III Forks employees, General Manager Rick Stein loves the restaurant. As far as he's concerned, there's no bad seat. "All our dining rooms have their charm. The main room is where you can easily be seen. If you want a quieter atmosphere, I suggest the Burnett Room next to the courtyard."

Opened in August 1998, III Forks serves dinner only, offering a menu of steaks and seafood—a land and sea mix dear to the heart of the 60-year old Wamstad. Nowhere is this depicted so dramatically than in the chandeliers in the main dining room (the Lafayette Room), which are crafted from elk antlers and feature women bow-spirits.

"These models of women bow-spirits graced the bows of clipper ships in the 17th, 18th, and 19th centuries," says Wamstad, who created the molds.

Soft lighting from the chandeliers casts a warm glow over the rooms, creating a warm, intimate and welcoming effect. Seated in this cozy room in red cushioned, dark-backed wooden chairs at finely set tables, customers can easily forget that they're dining in one of the largest restaurants in the country.

While the chandeliers are spectacular, they're just one of many splendid touches that makes a tour of III Forks *de rigueur*. It starts outside with the 24-karat-gold dome that sits high atop the restaurant, wooing visitors, whispering, "Come. Visit. I'm different."

*Stacy Hawkins and Lisa Webb check the evening's reservations. On a typical evening, III Forks may seat as many as 800 guests throughout the restaurant's twelve dining rooms.*

# There are only three such globes in existence, and Michael Eisner of Disney owns the other two…

Why a gold dome? "I just thought it would be great to do," explains Wamstad who remembered seeing one on a Masonic temple in News Orleans where he grew up.

A gold canopy over the entranceway enhances the gold theme and also reflects Wamstad's personal touch, which, from Del Frisco's to III Forks, has definitely been golden.

That gold dome also triggers fond memories among the III Forks staff. Chris Vogeli remembers getting up at 2 A.M. to help the construction workers put the dome on top of the restaurant. "It was stored in a flight hangar, and police cars escorted it through the streets of Addison into North Dallas. It was a thrill just to watch that big crane lift it up there."

The stained-glass front doors are tasteful and solid. Once in the lobby, visitors often pause a moment to examine the giant globe. It reflects the world of 1662, *Totius Terrarum Orbos*, as rendered by cartologist Dr. Joan Blaeu. If you're looking for the Atlantic Ocean it's the Mar Del Nort, the Gulf of Mexico is Goleo de Mexico and the Eastern seaboard is comprised of Virginia, Nova Britannia, and Nova Francia.

"I really like the globe," says Colleen. "That's kind of how Dale is. He saw a globe like that at the yacht club hotel in Disney World. He researched it, found out where it was made, and had one done special and shipped from England."

Wamstad adds that there are only three such globes in existence, and Michael Eisner of Disney owns the other two.

A glass cabinet in the hallway showcases a wedding dress and a saddle from a Cherokee Indian Princess, circa 1858. "That Native American dress and saddle were in our house for the longest time before this restaurant

*Live music is performed by a trio in the vestibule area off the main bar*

opened," adds Colleen, "so you know he had all this stuff charted out in his mind long before the building even started to go up."

A clipper ship display in another cabinet was inspired by a ship company in Baltimore. Nearby is a shoeshine stand, not your usual restaurant amenity, but a nice touch for busy executives.

Presiding over the stand is 63-year old Andrew Armstrong, who's been with Wamstad for twelve years and describes him as "one of the most straight-up guys I've ever worked for."

Armstrong averages about 20 shines a night. According to Pamela Landgraf, it's all part of the service. "Someone coming through the Dallas airport and running late for a meeting may end the day here for dinner. While waiting, he can have his shoes shined, something he may not have had a chance to do earlier."

A long curving bar sits to the right of the entrance, presided over by Bar Manager Danny Clopp and his team of bartenders. Next to it and looking directly into the sparkling clean kitchen is the Oyster Bar, great for a drink or for dinner amid the hubbub of the kitchen routine.

A Texas history buff, Wamstad wanted the state's 19th century battle for independence played out at III Forks. The dining rooms, for the most part, are named after figures in Texas history, mostly those who were at odds with Sam Houston at one time or another.

*Andrew Armstrong (above) presides over the shoeshine stand (right) near the entrance*

The Austin Room, partially hidden in the back of the first floor, is among Colleen's favorites. "It has a true old West, Big Valley kind of feel."

The room is named after Stephen F. Austin, a hero of the Texas Revolution with Mexico and considered the founder of Anglo-American Texas. He died in 1836, a young man at 43.

Colleen is also partial to the Captain's Room, presided over by Waiter-in-Charge Steve Tufts. Ideal for corporate parties, this room seats a maximum of 25 and features several attractive wine displays along the walls, plus full audio-visual support, including a video monitor and VCR equip-

*Director of Sales Pamela Landgraf
and Head Waiter Steve Tufts with a group
of diners in the Captain's Room*

ment for company presentations. This room is booked for months in advance.

A restaurant veteran with 25 years experience, Tufts, like so many others at III Forks, was working at Del Frisco's when he got to know Wamstad.

As III Forks was being built, Tufts had moved from Del Frisco's to manage a French bakery in Dallas. "It was a good job but starting every day at 4 A.M. got pretty rough."

Weary from lack of sleep, Tufts was receptive when Chris Vogeli's wife spotted him at the bakery. "Steve, did you know Dale is building out in III Forks. You might want to take a look," said Leslie Vogeli, looking out for her friend.

Knowing that Wamstad had a Midas touch with restaurants, Tufts was intrigued. "When he started something new, I felt it would be pretty colossal and wanted to be part of it."

When he got to the job site, Tufts asked, "Have you got anything for me?"

"If you want to work, you've got a job," Wamstad replied.

Shortly after III Forks opened in 1998, Rick Stein approached Tufts. "The Captain's Room is your new home. Make it work."

And he has. The room is booked almost nightly with some type of corporate meeting, function or private party. "For me the corporate meetings are the most exciting because you've got some pretty important deals going down in here," Tufts adds.

According to Tufts, Wamstad is still the consummate mom-and-pop owner. "It's the personal touch. I've talked to guests who might have met him twenty years ago in Louisiana and have followed him around to his restaurants."

Across from the Captain's Room is the Burnett Room, which is named after David G. Burnett, best remembered

as the president of the interim government of the Republic of Texas in the 1830s.

This dining room also opens into the main area, the Lafayette Room. Both the Burnett and Lafayette Rooms are distinguished by their elegant chandeliers.

The Lafayette Room is named after the Marquis de Lafayette. Although not involved in the Texas revolution, Lafayette was nevertheless a distinguished soldier and statesman who fought for liberty in both the American and French revolutions.

However, the murals ringing this room are distinctly Texan. "They depict the history of Texas from 1822 to this day," explains Wamstad. "All are on canvas except the corners because we couldn't bend the canvas."

But, in his typical "do-it-right" fashion, Wamstad had the corners plastered and then brought the artist back to paint on the plaster.

Lisa Webb works three days a week as Assistant Banquet Manager with Pamela Landgraf. "Dale's kind of like Scotch—an acquired taste. He can be difficult to work for, but you have to understand what he's driving at. He can be very vocal about his displeasure, but inside he's got a marshmallow heart."

In Webb's opinion, III Forks has a style all its own—an energy that sets it apart from other restaurants. "It's big, grandiose, and different from anything else, just like Dale."

To the right of the main lobby are two other dining rooms. The Fannin Room, with decorative Western saddles sitting on the dividers, is named for James W. Fannin who valiantly led troops in Texas' battle for independence from Mexico.

Next to the Fannin Room and opposite the wine cellar and humidor case, which holds up to 60 varieties of cigars, is the Sherman Room. It is named after Colonel Sydney William Sherman, a Kentuckian who led the left flank at the Battle of San Jacinto. It was Sherman who uttered the famous battle cry, "Remember the Alamo!"

# With its abundant greenery and elegant fountains, dining in the courtyard is like sitting under the stars.

Every day, these rooms, as well as the others, are scrutinized by Tierney Jory who opens the building in the morning.

Although she had been a corporate buyer for 15 years with J.C. Penney, Jory always loved the foodservice business. "I wanted to work in the best restaurant in town so I interviewed with Dale."

She started as a server and eventually became the office manager, taking care of banking, billing, accounting, payroll, morning inspections,

calling repair people, and occasionally taking a turn as the evening entertainer.

From morning on, she watches III Forks gather momentum for its 5 o'clock opening. "I like coming here in the morning. It's quiet and the lights are off. As the day progresses, things start to build. The kitchen crew comes in, then the floor managers."

According to Jory, each of the 12 dining rooms has its own energy level. "When they're all filled, this place really rocks. I remember when we had 23 banquets in one night last December."

Down the hall to the left, the courtyard sits slightly apart from the rest of III Forks. Once it was an outdoor seating area, but is now covered for year-round use. But, thanks to a light-colored ceiling, abundant greenery, elegant fountains, an eternal gas-burning flame, and patio flooring, the effect is almost like sitting under the stars.

A carpeted stairway leads to the second floor where the Promenade seats 100 and faces a stage for entertainers. On Saturdays and some evenings when parties are booked, a jazz band or some other musical group will perform here.

The upstairs bar is off to the left. Up a few stairs is the secluded Deaf Smith Room. This area is named for Erastus "Deaf" Smith, who, despite being hearing impaired, was one of the most effective scouts during Texas' fight for independence. Like the Captain's Room on the first floor, the

# Each of the twelve dining rooms has its own energy level…

Deaf Smith Room is much sought-after for high-powered boardroom-style dinners.

The other three second-floor rooms—all expandable from 30 to 50 seats—are ideal for business meetings, reunions, and other special occasions. Again, each is named for a significant figure in Texas history. For example, the Lamar Room is named for Mirabeau B. Lamar, a Georgian who came to Texas in 1835 in the midst of the revolution, rose from private to major general and eventually became the second president of the Republic of Texas after Sam Houston.

Next door is the Travis Room, honoring William Barrett Travis. For almost two weeks in 1836 at the Alamo, Lieutenant Colonel Travis and his company of 180 heroic Texans held off an invading Mexican army of more than 4,000 soldiers. On March 6, with no ammunition left, this tiny band used their muskets as clubs while fighting to the end. Although they all died, Travis' men had held the fort long enough for General Sam Houston to muster an army and attack the Mexicans. Spurred by Colonel Sydney Sherman's battle cry, "Remember the Alamo," Houston drove the invaders back across the border, saving independence for Texas.

Adjoining the Travis Room is the Bonham Room, named for another courageous Texan, J.D. Bonham, who fought his way into the Alamo to stand and die with Travis' soldiers.

Tucked in the back of the second floor is the Poker Room. While it lacks the historical panache of the other III Forks dining areas, this area is always a hit with customers. It seats from 8 to 12 and is actually Wamstad's office with a roll-top desk in one corner.

Reached through a small hallway near the upstairs pantry, this intimate gathering place could be the quintessential "smoke-filled" room—a secluded setting for backroom deals, hush-hush meetings, and confidential tête-a-têtes. And who's to say that doesn't happen? But mostly it's a very secluded place for dining with close friends and associates.

"People love eating there because it's so exclusive and intimate," says Landgraf. "There aren't many places where you can sit down with just a few friends in perfect quiet and enjoy a meal like this."

The room is also a favorite destination for Wamstad's children when they visit and roam through the restaurant. "They always head for the Poker Room," says Colleen of her exuberant brood.

Another of Colleen's favorite features is the bathroom. "It's beautiful and plush, and you can still hear the music from the floor. Plus, no one can believe that there's actually a baby's changing station in the ladies' room. You don't often find that in a restaurant like this."

Landgraf adds that, "People initially can't find the bathrooms because Dale did such a beautiful job of hiding them. Then I'll have guests rave about the big fluffy towels and the marble tops. Dale did the best with everything."

In her role as liaison with meeting planners, Landgraf hears all the feedback on III Forks. "People get pampered here. We had a group of Marriott chefs the other night who were awestruck by the place and stunned by the food."

Before joining the staff, Landgraf, the National Director of Sales, sold computers and insurance. She had to learn the restaurant business from square one.

"What I do now is actually quite similar to my previous jobs because I'm working with people and selling III Forks," she explains. With Wamstad as her tutor, Landgraf says she's learned from the master. "He's got a fantastic presence when he walks into a room. He's a perfect salesman who treats everyone like they were at his home for dinner."

Dallas is a thriving city for corporate parties and meetings, and III Forks gets more than its share. "We're usually super busy from Monday through Thursday for corporate events," Landgraf observes. "Then on Friday and Saturday they come back socially."

For Landgraf, nothing beats the "wow" that people experience when visiting III Forks. "It's always fun to make an impression with customers, many of whom run companies worth millions and millions of dollars. They bring in people who've never been here, and those people

*Dale Wamstad dines with his family, from left, daughter Dale Frances, wife Colleen, son Dane, and daughter Shelby in the upstairs Poker Room*

# Rick Stein Has It Covered

In her early days at III Forks, National Director of Sales Pamela Landgraf admits she would get nervous when parties she booked came to the restaurant. "I was new and not sure how things would turn out. Now I have confidence because everything about this place is perfect, and the staff is totally dedicated."

She cites General Manager Rick Stein as an example. "He's great to work with. If I can't figure out a table arrangement, he will, because he knows this business so well."

A veteran of fine-dining restaurants like Sam & Harry's Steak House in Washington, D.C. and Morton's of Chicago, Stein was a waiter at Del Frisco's in 1994 when he first met Wamstad. "He came in and smiled and was full of life. We hit if off right away."

When Wamstad left Del Frisco's in 1995, some of the restaurant's energy seemed to leave with him, says the 43-year-old Stein who himself decided to leave. "Dale just happened to stop by on my last shift. I thanked him for treating me well when he was here. He said 'I don't know where you're going, but I'm coming back for you.'"

"Heck I would have been a busboy for him. I really liked his style. He gave me the general manager position right from the start, and I was working here several months before we opened, helping to make some of the decisions about how we do things."

A native of Washington, D.C., Stein grew up in the towns of Rockville and Silver Springs, Maryland. He attended the University of Maryland, focusing on art.

Stein was a waiter in a number of restaurants, including Sam & Harry's. "They're still there and

doing a great job," he says, recalling the year he spent at the upscale steak house—a year that, as it turned out, changed his life.

One evening, Stein was tending bar. Although the place was packed, one particular lady caught his eye. "I never dated the clientele, but this was love at first sight," he explains of the chance encounter with the woman who would become his wife.

Tammy was from Dallas, visiting a cousin in Rockville, so Stein kept up a long distance romance before finally moving to the Lone Star State in 1991. Today, Tammy and Rick have a four-year-old daughter, Danielle, and one-year-old son, Josh.

As the general manager, Stein is ultimately responsible for everything at III Forks, answering to Dale and Gene Street. In the evening, in addition to Stein keeping an alert eye on all aspects of the dining rooms, every room has a floor manager overseeing the clientele and making sure that regulars and special parties are recognized.

Stein says, "You just never know who's going to walk in here—a politician, a sports figure, an actor, someone famous. It's always exciting."

Working for Wamstad can also be exhilarating. "He's a very fair guy," says Stein.

Like Wamstad, Stein feels that customers "should enjoy the experience of being here, and they should leave feeling that they got their money's worth."

Stein will tell you he doesn't take any day at III Forks for granted. "Not a day goes by when I don't pull up and see that big dome and think, 'Wow, look where I'm headed. I'm lucky someone like Dale found me and appreciated my work ethic."

That work ethic is hidden behind a broad smile and genial nature that makes Stein easy to like. In fact, it's hard to imagine anyone better suited to making customers feel at home than this III Forks general manager.

# Ask anyone who's been to III Forks, and they'll mention a favorite room…

will tell someone else, 'Hey, this is where we were the other night, and it was great.'"

At this point, Landgraf holds up a small green velvet bag and draws out a heavy gold coin with the restaurant's logo. "This is another unique III Forks touch. These are our gift certificates. Instead of paper, we sell these coins in denominations from $20 to $250 for dinner or drinks here."

This Wamstad idea has had amazing success. "People love the way they look. They're different," Landgraf says. "It's been a phenomenon. And there's no expiration date. Do you know how great that makes the customer feel?"

Ask anyone who's been to III Forks, and they'll mention a favorite room. For Gene Street, it's the Lafayette Room. "It's gorgeous with the chandeliers and all the artwork."

Also high on Street's list is the Poker Room. "A lot of the celebrities like it because of the privacy," he notes.

Eleana Jones, Chief Financial Officer for Consolidated Restaurant Operations, loves the wine cellar. "It's a beautiful little room with the most incredible light fixture. It just shows that attention to detail that Dale put into III Forks."

## *III Forks*

---

CHAPTER SIX

# FOOD & RECIPES FROM III FORKS

*E*very menu at III Forks carries this notation: "Attitude is everything and the eye of the master will fatten the calf."

This reference to the dedication to quality of a vanishing breed—the independent cattleman—is attributed to Captain Bob Cooper in 1838. Cooper, who changed his name from Beau Coup to avoid being exported to New Orleans as a Frenchman during the Texas-Mexican Revolution, was a legendary cook, recipe maker, and cooking instructor. Some have called him "the father of true American cooking."

A look at the history of Texas food is part of a book compiled for III Forks by Executive Chef Chris Vogeli. Bound in cowhide, this massive volume also contains more than 275 recipes from III Forks, some of which are reproduced here, as well as photographs of some of the extraordinary cuisine featured on the restaurant's menu.

# Banana Bread Pudding

1 cup evaporated milk

1 cup milk

10 slices raisin bread

4 oz. butter, melted

1 cup sugar

3 eggs

3 ripe bananas, mashed

1 teaspoon vanilla

$1/2$ teaspoon salt

1 teaspoon cinnamon

$1/4$ teaspoon nutmeg

1. Scald the milk and evaporated milk together in a heavy saucepan. Set aside.

2. In a large mixing bowl, combine the remaining ingredients. Add the scalded milk and stir to mix all the ingredients thoroughly.

3. Pour the mixture into a buttered baking dish. Bake at 350°F for approximately 30 minutes.

# Bananas Foster

YIELD: 8 SERVINGS

8 bananas

1 cup unsalted butter

2 cups brown sugar, packed

1 cup dark rum

2 quarts of vanilla ice cream (preferably homemade)

1. Peel the bananas and cut into halves.

2. In a large sauté pan, melt the butter and add the brown sugar. Place the bananas on top. Cook for 5 minutes on medium heat until brown sugar melts and forms a sauce.

3. Remove the pan from the heat and add the rum. Return the pan to the stove and gently heat the rum.

4. Remove from stove and using a long fireplace matchstick, light the rum to flame.

5. Carefully place back on the stove to cook until flame goes out. Shake the pan to blend sauce.

6. Remove bananas and place over ice cream. Mix sauce to smooth using a fork and ladle sauce over bananas. Serve immediately.

# Mushroom Sauté

YIELD: 8 PORTIONS

1 cup unsalted butter

$1/4$ cup onions, chopped finely

2 pounds button mushrooms, washed

1 tablespoon garlic, minced

$1/2$ cup white wine

2 teaspoons salt

$1/4$ teaspoon ground black pepper

2 tablespoons fresh parsley, finely chopped

1. Melt the butter in a heavy skillet. Add the garlic, onions and mushrooms. Saute over medium heat, stirring constantly for 5 minutes.

2. Add the wine and reduce until almost dry. Season with salt and pepper. Sprinkle in chopped parsley. Serve immediately.

# Crab Cakes

1 pound fresh lump crab meat

1 extra large egg, lightly beaten

$1/2$ cup mayonnaise

$1/2$ teaspoon dry mustard

2 teaspoons Worcestershire sauce

$1/2$ cup green pepper, (finely diced)

$1/4$ cup pimento, (medium diced)

1 tablespoon chopped parsley

$1^{1}/2$ cups fresh bread crumbs (crust removed)

1 teaspoon crushed red pepper

1. Combine all the ingredients and mix lightly. Form into cakes 2–3 inches in diameter.

2. Fry or pan sauté.

# Beef and Potato Salad

2 whole dill pickles, diced

2 medium red onions, chopped

2 medium potatoes, peeled, diced and cooked

2 lbs. cooked beef tenderloin, cubed

2 oz. pickle juice

2 oz. red wine vinegar

3 oz. extra-virgin olive oil

2 tablespoons black pepper

1 tablespoon salt

1. Toss all ingredients together and refrigerate. Serve chilled on a bed of bibb lettuce.

# III Forks Off-the-Cob Cream Corn

Yield: 12 servings

10 ears fresh corn, cooked and cut off the cob

1 cup heavy cream

1 cup milk

2 tablespoons sugar

1 teaspoon kosher salt

$^1/_2$ teaspoon white pepper

$^1/_2$ teaspoon black pepper

$^1/_4$ teaspoon Accent

$^1/_2$ teaspoon granulated garlic

$^1/_2$ teaspoon thyme

4 oz. salted butter

2 tablespoons flour

1. In a stockpot, combine the first 10 ingredients. Slowly bring it to a boil. Reduce to a simmer. Allow to simmer for 3 minutes.

2. In a separate saucepan, bring the butter to a boil. Stir in the flour. Add butter and flour mixture to the simmering corn.

3. Stirring occasionally, allow to simmer for 3 more minutes. Keep warm until serving.

# III Forks Sauce

*Great with fish and other seafood.*

YIELD: 24 OZ. (8 - 3 OZ. SERVINGS)

1 pint heavy cream

4 oz. butter

Pinch cayenne pepper

1/4 teaspoon white pepper

2 teaspoons flour

2 teaspoons warm water

1/2 teaspoon salt

2 oz. butter

1/2 bunch green onions

1/2 teaspoon coarse black pepper

1/4 teaspoon oregano

1/4 teaspoon thyme

1/4 teaspoon basil

3 cloves of garlic

1 oz. capers

1 tablespoon parsley

1 tablespoon lemon juice

1 peeled and chopped tomato

1. In a thick-bottomed saucepot, bring heavy cream to a boil and simmer until reduced by one-third in volume.

2. In a skillet, cook the butter until foamy and add to the reduced cream. Make a white wash by combining the cayenne pepper, white pepper, flour, and water and add to the cream mixture. Whisk sauce occasionally to keep from scorching.

3. In a skillet, sauté the green onion in butter for 2 minutes on medium heat. Add the garlic and black pepper. Sauté for 1 minute, and add to the cream sauce.

4. Add the oregano, thyme, basil, tomato, parsley, and lemon juice. Bring sauce back to a boil and remove from heat. Keep warm until needed.

# Grilled Campfire Trout

Two 8-oz. trout filets

4 tablespoons butter

2 teaspoons salt

Pinch ground black pepper

Pinch ground white pepper

2 tablespoons parsley, chopped

4 tablespoons unsalted butter

4 tablespoons pecan pieces

1/4 teaspoon salt

Juice of 1/2 lemon

Juice of 1/2 orange

Worcestershire sauce

1. Season fish with salt and pepper.

2. In a large sauté pan, melt the butter. Pan fry trout, cooking 3 minutes per side or until opaque and cooked through. Remove trout to serving plate.

3. In the same pan, add the remaining butter, parsley, and pecans. Sauté until butter is foamy brown.

4. Add salt, lemon juice, orange juice, and Worcestershire sauce. Remove sauce from heat and pour over trout. Serve immediately.

# Beefsteak Tomato Salad

YIELD: 8 SERVINGS

8 beefsteak tomatoes

**RED ONION VINAIGRETTE**

1 pound red onion, sliced thin

2 tablespoons kosher salt

2 teaspoons ground black pepper

³/₄ cup red wine vinegar

2 cups olive oil

¹/₄ cup fresh basil, chopped

¹/₄ cup fresh parsley, chopped

1. In a large mixing bowl, combine all the ingredients except tomatoes. Mix well, cover, and refrigerate until needed.

2. When ready to serve the tomato salad, cut the tomatoes at the very last moment into ¹/₂-inch-thick slices and place on small chilled plates. Drizzle the dressing over the tomatoes.

**NOTE:** 1 oz. of crumbled blue cheese on top of each accompanies this salad well.

# Remoulade Sauce

4 large spoons of mayonnaise

2 large spoonfuls of Creole mustard

1 tablespoon horseradish

5 shakes of Worcestershire sauce

3 shakes of Tabasco sauce

Juice of three lemons

1 bunch of celery stalks, chopped fine

1 large spoon of garlic powder

1 large spoon of white pepper

1 large spoon of salt

Paprika to color

1. Mix all the ingredients together well and chill for several hours before serving.

# Peach Custard

4 heaping teaspoons of all purpose flour

1 extra large egg

1 cup sugar

1¹/₂ cups milk

Pinch of salt

¹/₂ teaspoon vanilla extract

6 large fresh peaches

1. In a saucepan, over medium heat, cook flour, egg, sugar, milk, and salt until thick, stirring constantly. Stir in vanilla extract.

2. Peel peaches, cut into eighths, and place in a large mixing bowl. Place warm sauce over peaches. Place in refrigerator, covered, for 12 hours. Serve in stemmed serving dish topped with whipped cream.

## Whipped Cream

1 cup heavy cream

¹/₄ cup sugar

¹/₂ teaspoon vanilla extract

1. Combine all the ingredients in the bowl of a mixer. Whip until thick.

# Veal Oscar with Crab and Asparagus Hollandaise

4 pieces of 4 oz. veal scaloppini steaks

4 tablespoons of all purpose flour

1/4 teaspoon salt

Pinch cayenne pepper

1/8 teaspoon of ground white pepper

1/8 teaspoon of ground black pepper

4 tablespoons butter

2 oz. white wine

2 tablespoons unsalted butter, chilled

2 teaspoons chopped chives

2 teaspoons chopped parsley

4 oz. lump crabmeat, well picked and cleaned

6 pieces jumbo asparagus, blanched

1/2 teaspoon salt

1 recipe Hollandaise Sauce

1. Dust veal scaloppini steaks with flour. Season with salt and peppers.

2. Heat butter in an iron skillet over medium heat. Add the veal scaloppini and cook 30 seconds per side. The veal should not brown but actually stay white. Remove veal from pan and place on a warmed serving plate.

3. Pour off excess fat and deglaze the pan with the white wine, reducing the wine by half.

4. Add the crabmeat, asparagus, butter, chives, parsley. Reduce heat just to warm ingredients and melt the butter. Arrange ingredients neatly on top of veal and pour sauce over the top. Place a dollop of hollandaise on top just before serving.

# Hollandaise Sauce

YIELD: 1 QUART

6 egg yolks

1 teaspoon salt

1/8 teaspoon cayenne pepper

1/8 teaspoon ground white pepper

2 tablespoons sherry wine

1 teaspoon Worcestershire sauce

1/4 teaspoon Tabasco sauce

1 tablespoon lemon juice

2 tablespoons warm water

24 oz. clarified butter (warmed to 100°F)

2 tablespoons Creole mustard

2 tablespoons warm water

1. In a 4-quart mixing bowl, add egg yolks, salt, peppers, wine, lemon juice, Worcestershire sauce, and Tabasco sauce.

2. Place bowl over a hot pot of water (a *bain-marie*) and whisk steadily to cook the egg yolk mixture. When the egg yolk mixture becomes pale yellow and thickens like custard, remove from heat.

3. Slowly whisk in about a third of the clarified butter. If the sauce begins to look too thick or too shiny at any point during this process, thin it down with a little water. Continue to add the clarified butter in a steadier stream until all the butter is added.

4. Stir in Creole mustard. Season to taste with lemon juice and more additional salt if desired. Keep in a warm place, covered, until needed.

# Steak au Poivre

Two 12 oz. boneless strip steaks, $1/2$-inch thick

2 tablespoons butter

2 tablespoons whole black pepper (crush with a rolling pin)

2 tablespoons kosher salt

2 tablespoons unsalted butter

2 tablespoons cognac

2 oz. Worcestershire sauce

1 tablespoon A-1 sauce

2 tablespoons chopped parsley

1 tablespoon chopped chives

2 teaspoons lemon juice

4 oz. heavy cream

1. Combine two tablespoons of the butter, crushed black peppercorns, and kosher salt. Press into the steaks and let stand for 20 minutes.

2. Melt the additional butter in a heavy iron skillet. Cook the steaks in the butter on high heat until well browned on one side, then turn over. For medium or well-done steaks, reduce the heat. When steak is cooked to desired temperature, remove from skillet and let stand on a serving plate.

3. Pour off the grease from the skillet. Return the skillet to heat and add cognac, Worcestershire sauce, A-1 sauce, parsley, chives, lemon juice, and heavy cream. Reduce the sauce to thicken, pour over steaks, and serve.

# Sugar Snap Peas

YIELD: 8 SERVINGS

$1^{1}/_{2}$ lb. sugar snap peas

4 oz. butter, unsalted

1 tablespoon garlic, freshly chopped

1 teaspoon salt

$1/_2$ teaspoon black pepper

1. In a large saucepan, bring 2 quarts of water and 1 tablespoon of salt to a boil. Add snap peas and allow to cook for 1½ minutes. Drain the peas and remove to a covered serving dish to keep warm.

2. While the saucepan is still hot, add the butter and garlic. Stir, allowing the butter to melt and begin to pop.

3. Stir in the sugar snap peas and season with salt and pepper. Serve immediately.

# Snickerdoodles

YIELD: 24 LARGE COOKIES

1 cup butter, unsalted

3 cups all purpose flour

2 cups sugar

2 eggs

1 teaspoon vanilla extract

½ teaspoon baking soda

½ teaspoon cream of tartar

**CINNAMON SUGAR COATING**

1 cup sugar

1 tablespoon ground cinnamon

1. Cream the butter in a mixing bowl. Add 1 cup of the flour, the sugar, eggs, vanilla extract, baking soda, and cream of tartar. Beat until smooth. Beat in the remaining flour just to combine.

2. Place the dough on a large piece of parchment or wax paper. Form into a cylinder that is 3 inches in diameter and roll tightly in the paper. Refrigerate for 1 hour.

3. Remove dough from the refrigerator and cut into ½-inch-thick slices. Place the cinnamon-sugar mixture in a deep pie pan. Coat each of the cookies well with the cinnamon-sugar mixture and place on an ungreased cookie sheet.

4. Bake at 350°F for 12 minutes or until the edges turn lightly brown. Cool cookies on wire racks and place in an airtight container at room temperature.

# Roasted Tomato Basil Soup

14 Roma tomatoes

3 strips smoked bacon

1 oz. olive oil

1 large onion, chopped

2 stalks celery, chopped

10 cloves garlic, chopped

1 bay leaf

1 tablespoon thyme

3 oz. tomato paste

4 oz. white wine

1 pint fresh tomatoes, diced

1 gallon chicken stock

1 tablespoon salt

Fresh basil, chopped

Salt and black pepper, to taste

Chopped parsley (optional)

Croutons (optional)

1. Place the Roma tomatoes on a sheet pan and roast in a 350°F oven for 30 minutes. Remove and set aside.

2. In a large stock pot over medium-high heat, render the bacon in the olive oil. Add the onions, celery and garlic. Sauté until translucent, then stir in the thyme, bay leaves, and tomato paste.

3. Deglaze with the white wine, then add the tomato scraps, roasted Roma tomatoes, chicken stock, and 1 tablespoon salt. Bring to a boil, reduce to a simmer, and allow to cook for 25 minutes.

4. Puree the soup in small batches in a blender and strain. Season to taste with basil, salt, and pepper. If desired, garnish each serving with a few croutons and some chopped parsley.

# Sweet Potato Pie

MAKES 2 NINE-INCH PIES

5 large eggs, beaten

3 cups cooked sweet potatoes

2 cups sugar

1 teaspoon salt

2 teaspoons cinnamon

1 teaspoon ground ginger

3$^1/_2$ cups half-and-half

1. In a mixing bowl, combine the eggs and sweet potato; mix together well.

2. Add the sugar, salt, cinnamon, and ginger, and stir to combine. Stir in the half-and-half and mix until all the ingredients are well combined.

3. Divide the filling into the two pie shells. Bake at 375°F for 1 hour. Remove from oven and let pies cool. Whip the heavy cream with additional sugar until stiff peaks. Serve Chantilly Cream on the side.

# Chantilly Cream

1 pint heavy cream

1 teaspoon vanilla

$^1/_2$ cup sugar

1. Combine all ingredients and whip until light and fluffy.

# Pie Dough

MAKES 2 NINE-INCH PIES

4$^1/_2$ cups cake or pastry flour

$^1/_4$ teaspoon salt

$^1/_2$ cup sugar

1$^1/_2$ cups unsalted butter, cut into small cubes

2 extra large eggs

3 extra large egg yolks

1. In a mixing bowl, combine the pastry flour, sugar, and salt; mix well. Add the butter. Using a fork, cut the butter into the flour until it resembles course cornmeal consistency.

2. Add the eggs and egg yolks and continue to mix until dough forms. Wrap in plastic and refrigerate until needed. To use, remove from the refrigerator and let come to room temperature. Dough can be rolled out or actually pressed into pie pans.

Note: For chocolate dough, add 1 cup of cocoa (unsweetened). For spiced dough, add ¼ teaspoon of cinnamon, nutmeg, or ground ginger to flour mixture at the beginning of the recipe.

# Venison with Sweet Potato Pancakes

Two 8 oz. venison sirloin steaks, ¹/₂-inch thick

1 tablespoon whole black pepper (crush with a rolling pin)

2 teaspoons kosher salt

1 tablespoon unsalted butter

1 additional tablespoon of unsalted butter

2 oz. finely diced onions

1 teaspoon garlic, chopped

4 oz. diced apples (peeled and seeded)

2 oz. red wine vinegar

4 oz. heavy cream

1 tablespoon chopped parsley

2 teaspoons chopped tarragon

2 tablespoons unsalted butter, chilled

1. Press salt and pepper mix into the steak. Let stand 20 minutes.

2. In a heavy iron skillet, sauté the venison in butter on high flame until well-browned on one side, then flip. For medium or well-done steaks, reduce heat. When steak is cooked to desired temperature, remove from skillet and let stand on a serving plate.

3. Pour off the grease from the skillet. Return the skillet to heat and add the butter, onions, garlic, and apples. Sauté until the onions become translucent, approximately 3 minutes.

4. Add the red wine vinegar and tarragon, and reduce until nearly dry. Add the heavy cream and parsley, and reduce the sauce to thicken.

5. Whisk in the 2 tablespoons butter off the fire and pour the completed sauce over the steaks. Serve with Sweet Potato Pancakes (recipe follows).

## Sweet Potato Pancakes

*Perfect to serve with venison steaks.*

1 pound large sweet potatoes, peeled and grated

¹/₂ pound medium baking potatoes, peeled and grated

¹/₂ medium yellow onion, grated

1 egg, lightly beaten

1 tablespoon fresh bread crumbs

1 teaspoon salt

¹/₂ teaspoon freshly ground black pepper

2 tablespoons maple syrup

Pinch of grated fresh nutmeg

2 tablespoons of all purpose flour

4 oz. clarified butter to cook pancakes

1. Place the potatoes and onions in a colander, rinse with cold water, and drain thoroughly.

2. In a mixing bowl, combine the drained potatoes and all remaining ingredients, except oil. Divide the mixture into 8 portions and drain again. Pat each portion into a flat cake about ½-inch thick.

3. In a large skillet, heat the oil to medium-high heat. Cook the pancakes until browned, 4 to 5 minutes. Turn the pancakes and cook on the other side until golden brown and crispy. Remove pancakes to paper towels to drain. Keep warm in aluminum foil until ready to serve.

# Index